"REAL LIVES IN A REAL WORLD"

CARLOS CAMACHO, COMPILER

Pacific Press® Publishing Association
Nampa, Idaho
Oshawa, Ontario, Canada
www.pacificpress.com

Editor: Miguel Valdivia
Cover design: Gerald Lee Monks
Cover illustration: Milton Coronado
Inside design: Aaron Troia

Copyright © 2009 by
Pacific Press® Publishing Association
P. O. Box 5353, Nampa, Idaho 83653
Printed in the United States of America
All rights reserved

Additional copies of this book are available by calling toll-free 1-800-765-6955 or by
visiting http://www.adventistbookcenter.com.

PUBLICACIONES
ADVENTISTAS DEL 7° DIA

ISBN 13: 978-0-8163-9322-0
ISBN 10: 0-8163-9322-2

09 10 11 12 • 4 3 2

CONTENTS

José Vicente Rojas   *Introduction* 4

Gustavo Sánchez   *From Tragedy to Hope* 7

Carlos Acosta   *From a "Vato Loco" to a "Vato Loco 4 Jesus"* 21

Harold Altamirano   *Rebel Heart* 33

Yami Bazán   *Answering the Call: A Journey of Faith*....................44

Milton Coronado   *Tagged By God* 55

José Cortés   *Is There Really a Heaven?*..66

Manny Cruz   *What God Sees In You* 80

José Marín   *Your Ultimate Purpose*...87

Elden Ramírez   *God Does Not Waste Your Pain* 100

Sergio Torres   *A Walnut Tree and a Church in the Front Yard*...... 111

Willie Ramos   *When You Are Down To Nothing,*
God Is Up To Something 122

Glossary 128

INTRODUCTION

JOSÉ VICENTE ROJAS

Have you ever been inside a courtroom? Those of us who have spent time explaining ourselves to the law have learned a few things about courtrooms. The first thing that sticks with you is that when you appear before the judge, you usually only get one chance to make your case and convince the judge that you are innocent.

The entire process of the courtroom hearing or trial hinges on the absolute necessity of witnesses who place their right hand on a Bible and, as they lift their left hand, swear to, "tell the truth, the whole truth, and nothing but the truth."

You will find that "hearsay" is not allowed in court. Hearsay is when you tell something that you heard from others. There is no courtroom that allows a witness to tell what someone else told them. The ONLY testimony that is allowed in a courtroom is when a witness tells strictly what they have *experienced*.

This is why you will find today that the most powerful thing you can ever do is to tell what you have experienced personally. Your most precious friends have been people who are honest and tell you what they see and experience in their lives. Your favorite boss has probably been someone who actually worked at your job and mastered it to the point of becoming a leader. Your favorite sermons have probably been preached by speakers who were not afraid to be transparent about what they have seen in their lives and how this applies to today.

The power of a testimony in the Bible brought many people to a saving knowledge of God. When Jesus preached to the masses, healed people, or liberated them from evil, He would tell them to "go and tell your friends and family what you have seen." To another person He said, "Go and tell others what great things God has done for you and how much mercy He's shown you!" As a result of the testimonies of those who had experienced Jesus in their lives, thousands more followed Him!

A testimony will change the lives of those who hear it because the testimony is proof that God is with us. Testimonies confirm that God is near; that if God can bless "that guy or that girl, He can also bless me." Testimonies give hope to those who thought there was no hope left. A testimony indeed brings hope to the "courtroom" of life.

The chapters in this book are written by a group of some of the most blessed and fruitful Latino youth leaders in North America. They are pastors, youth directors, and specialists in the challenges of living in a cross-cultural society. This crew of "attitude" Christian youth leaders has learned a lot from their walk with God.

As you read these pages, you will find that they are open and honest about their journeys. You will laugh with them, cry with them, and look toward heaven with them as they testify only to what they have seen in their lives with Jesus.

Read these stories of courage testifying to the power of God to transform a life that now impacts others for Christ. Some of these writers came from the streets, others from sheltered homes, still others from poverty and great want. But all come together in this book to confirm that God truly has a plan for each one of us.

Each author has shown a special way of testifying, as if they have each written with their right hand on a Bible, and in these pages have committed to telling the truth, the whole truth, and nothing but the truth, as God has helped them.

Read for yourself and see that God is exonerated through the testimonies of His people!

—The author is director of Volunteer Services for the Seventh-day Adventist Church in North-America, and a well-known international speaker.

The stories were compiled by Carlos Camacho, a youth pastor from Southern California, who now serves as director of International Sales at Pacific Press, in Nampa, Idaho.

GUSTAVO SÁNCHEZ

I got out of the truck not realizing what had happened. My daughter, who was standing by the truck, was trying to tell me something, but I could not make it out. I knew something was terribly wrong from the terror I could see in her face. My wife ran out and started screaming; my little girl was still trying to speak … My other daughter (her twin sister) was dead, under my own truck! My world came tumbling down on me. I remember a police officer running over to get me away from my daughter. The next thing I remember is that we were hugging and crying together.

I—*El Génesis*

I was born on May 4, 1978, in Nampa, Idaho, to Roberto and Martha Sánchez. My mom lived in Eagle Pass, Texas, and would migrate to Idaho looking for work. Mom was a hard working woman from a very young age. She had to drop out of school to work in the fields to help her family to survive.

My grandpa was a field contractor. Every year Grandpa, Grandma, and all the kids would move to Idaho for the harvest season, then back to Texas. It was a pretty hard way of life because I was in and out of school, never being able to finish a complete year in one place. It was so bad that I flunked first grade for not being in school the minimum amount of days.

My mom and I lived with my grandparents. My dad left the scene and pretty much abandoned us for reasons unknown to me. Dad lived a hard life. He grew up poor in a border town. His dad, "La Cheetah," my grandpa, was an alcoholic and did not really contribute to the family. Grandpa was murdered on the streets of Eagle Pass. He was robbed and stabbed to death; so my dad and his siblings were forced to fend for themselves. Dad left home when he was twelve years old. He traveled by himself doing odd jobs in state after state.

Mom and I were really close. She was a very loving and caring mom. She was, and still is, my hero—the best mom in the world. I was about five years old when dad came back into our lives. It was a great thing, but it probably changed my life for the worse.

My dad, since I can remember, was a very violent man, dedicated to the gang life. He was a drug user and a heavy drinker. My dad was also involved in the drug-trafficking world. When I was about eight, we moved back to Nampa, Idaho. We moved because my dad was running from the cops. He had gotten himself involved in some trouble and we had to leave. We packed what we could in my dad's lowrider, a yellow 1977 Buick, and we left. By then my brother Robert had already been born. We moved to the northside, the worst part of Nampa, and there, three years later, my sister Lorena was born.

In Nampa, life did not improve. In fact, our lives became even bumpier. Mom met the Lord and became a religious woman. She came to understand that the life she and her family were leading was wrong. As my mom's lifestyle changed, so did what she tolerated in her home, which caused many fights between dad and her. Usually, the fight would end up with dad leaving or even us— Mom and kids—leaving. I still remember spending cold nights sleeping in the car because Dad would not leave.

Besides those fights, there was my dad's dependence on alcohol. Sometimes when he started drinking, he would leave and not come back home for three, six months, or even a year—sometimes longer if he ended up in jail or prison. As for me, all I wanted was my dad. I wanted somebody to talk to, somebody who would take care of us, who would take me fishing, or show me how to work on cars, but you know, it turned out differently.

As I was growing up, I was exposed to the life of gangs and drugs. I would see so many drug sales that one day, after a sale, I got into my dad's stash and took a joint. Then I went to my uncle's house and tried to sell it. I was about five years old at my first *transa* (transaction).

I was always terrified of Beto. Since I didn't know my dad until I was five, I never called him "Dad"; I referred to him by his nickname, "Beto." Beto was even more violent when he was drinking. As soon as he started drinking, my stomach would be tied up in a knot. He would go crazy, break in the house, and hurt my mom.

I remember one time when my mom and dad were fighting. There was lots of yelling, my brother Roberto and I hid and cried, afraid for my mom. The yelling turned to cries for help, then silence. My dad hit my mom so hard that he knocked her out. He started to panic. I don't think he had ever gone that far; I remember seeing the fear in his face. So, either because he got scared that the cops were coming or because he thought he might have killed her, he left. But before leaving, he gave us instructions. He grabbed a bottle of alcohol, and told us to put some of it on a towel and rub her face until she woke up. So there we were—I was nine, my brother was two—left alone to revive my mom.

Man, I can never forget that. We were crying, rubbing her face with the alcohol, and screaming at her to wake up. Finally she did. She was disoriented and did not remember much about what had happened, but she threw her arms around us and we just sat there and cried together.

Beto continued his life on the streets. Sometimes he would come home hurt and bleeding from a fight. On many other occasions, it was he who hurt others. One time our home was surrounded with *narcos* (cops who worked for the Narcotics Division) looking for my dad. I knew something bad had happened, and started asking around. There was a small store nearby where we lived, Friendly Fred's, and I found out that Dad had been there talking to some people, and this one guy kept bothering him. They say my dad went into the store, bought a knife, went out and sliced that guy's throat from ear to ear.

Now he was on the run. He contacted me and told me not to worry; he was fine and he would fix things. Luckily, the guy that got sliced made it. They had to staple his throat back together. Later, my dad was caught and taken to jail. He awaited trial, but for some reason, the victim did not show up at court and the charges were dropped.

Chaos seemed to be the only sure thing in our lives. Mom couldn't afford everything on her own, so we moved to the projects where she could get help. Because I was exposed to such degree of violence, my heart was filled with lots of anger and pain. I always wondered if I was loved or if somehow I had any fault in all of this. Why couldn't my dad just be a dad?

I also remember that I would always try to fix problems between Mom and Dad. I would find ways to get them back together. I would plead with my mom to let Dad back in. I would tell her that he would stop and change, to just give him another chance. It was soon after that my own life took a turn for the worse.

II—Life in the gang

Mom wanted to get out of the projects and dreamed of one day being able to buy her own house. Finally her dream came true. She bought a house about two blocks from where we were living and across the street from the projects, still in the *barrio*. I started to rebel when I was about twelve years old. Mom was really restricted on finances, barely making ends meet. So she couldn't pay for any of the extra things we wanted, like bikes, cool clothes, et cetera.

Remember that joint I tried to sell when I was five? I decided that this could be a source of income. So, I started selling at school. I would buy an "eight"—a twenty-dollar sack—break it into joints, and double my money. By that time, I also started to experiment with drugs and alcohol.

Man, I remember the first cigarette I smoked; it was the most disgusting thing I had ever done. Same with the first time I got drunk … man, it sucked! The whole world would start going in circles. You get all sick and throw up. But you know, I had to show that I could hang.

I started hanging out with the homeboys and was accepted into the gang. Now I was a Norteño XIV in one of the biggest gangs in the valley. They supplied the love and acceptance I was lacking at home. But among the memories, what happened to one of my closest homeboys stands out. He was a good *vato*. Unfortunately, he didn't make it.

One night we were going to throw a big party. All the homies were getting together and we were going to "jump" some new guys in. I got there early. Not much was happening yet. There was no beer, so I sent for a couple of beer kegs to get started. Lots of home-boys started showing up, and we started to party.

I was playing craps (dice) with some of the homies, and was bent down watching the dice, when everybody became quiet. I looked up and saw a blue '63 Impala creeping up on us. It happened very quickly: the passenger sat on the door jamb with his body halfway out the car, rested the 12-gauge on the roof, and started blasting. I froze for a split second, then realized that there were bullets flying by my head. I looked around and saw everybody hitting the floor. I ran and dived. As you can imagine, this changed the mood for the rest of the night. Later, we jumped some of the homies in, one of them was my cousin.

Later that night, another car came creeping up. We didn't know who they were and didn't care; they were bothering us, so we pulled out the *cohetes* (guns) and rang some warning shots. The party went on all night. I left at some point in the middle of the night or early morning. A few hours later, I heard of the tragic news. At some point in the early morning, some dudes showed up, broke into the house, and shot one of the guys seven times. Another homie was hit twice in the head.

Both lived, but that morning I lost my closest friend. When he was shot, he managed to get away and run, but they caught up to him and shot him again at close range. Somehow he managed to get to a relative's house. They put him in the car and started rushing him to the hospital. While in the car, all he could say was, "Tell my mom that I love her." And then he was gone.

At this point in my life, I had completely rebelled against my mom; she couldn't control me. I would leave for weeks. I was smoking weed, snorting cocaine, crank, and anything and everything I could get my hands on. As I grew older, my relationship with my dad was no longer a father-son relationship but a homeboy-partner relationship. A couple of years went by. I had been struggling at school but managed to pass ninth grade. That summer things got even worse.

My father was still leading the same lifestyle. He was still making easy money and I also became pretty good at it. We started working together; he started showing me the ropes, teaching me how to be a successful dealer. Every day I had to go home and unload the money because I could fit no more in my pockets. Sometimes, before I could show it to my dad and count it all out, I would have to wait till my mom left, since she never accepted this type of thing in her house. I would wait until she was gone to count the money in the living room. To me, it was the greatest satisfaction to see a big smile on my dad's face. From the pats on the back he would give me, I felt he was proud of me and loved me.

I learned that this lifestyle consisted of many laughs in public, and many secret tears behind closed doors. So, I learned to keep those tears as deep inside my soul as possible. Drugs and alcohol were my refuge. I would stay up for days. One time, believe it or not, I stayed up partying with no sleep for twenty-four days. I would drink and party all day and all night. My life was on a downhill spiral.

III—*Redimido* (Redeemed)

Next to the house that my mom bought lived a really nice family. It included a young beautiful girl my age, her name was Annette. We started talking; she became my girl and we moved together to a house in the *barrio* close to my mother's house. Soon Annette and I had a set of twins—Aliyah and Alicia—another daughter, Angelica, and finally my son, Tavo. Now I was a family man. Life seemed to be getting better. But my past would come back to haunt me.

Through all this, I was still leading the same lifestyle. I had slowed down on the drugs, but started to drink heavily. Pretty soon I was a full-blown alcoholic. I was drinking everyday all day. During the week, because I worked, I would drink at least a twelve-pack, and usually eighteen beers a day. On the weekends, I would drown myself.

I started getting blackouts and sometimes would be gone for days at a time. This started causing lots of fights at home. I got in trouble with the law and went to jail. I lost my job. At the same time, I was thinking of my family, thinking of what I was doing to them. I thought of how I grew up, and it dawned on me that I was repeating it in my children's lives. It was just chaos.

I started feeling lost, scared, alone, empty, and not even the alcohol would help anymore. There was something I needed but I didn't know what. I was searching for answers, but I didn't even know what to look for. To me, the answer was to run to my hiding spot: drugs and alcohol. My life once again was on a downward spiral.

But it would take a turn for the better. I would finally find the answer that I was looking for. My mother and I were always very close. She was always on me telling me to change. She constantly reminded me of the life we had with my father and how I was going down the same path. She would always talk to me about Jesus. She would always call me—every Friday—to invite me to go to church on Saturday, but I would tell her that church was not for me, or I would be sick (hungover) from my constant drinking.

It was Friday again. I finished work, stopped at the store like always, and picked up some beer. I got home and started getting ready to drink when the phone rang. I looked at the caller ID. I expected my mom, but it was a number I didn't recognize. I answered the phone and somebody said, "This is José Herrera, I'm from the Seventh-day Adventist church. We are having some meetings starting tonight, and I want to invite you to come."

My mom had gotten smarter. She knew how I was; she knew how hard it was for me to say "No" to somebody else. So, she had one of the members from her church call and invite me. I also wanted to get my mom off my back, so I agreed to go. Then my mom called to find out what had happened. She was excited that I was going. Then she told me what time she would be picking me up, and so she did.

Man, I was as nervous as if I was going to court. We got there; I had butterflies in my stomach. I was very uncomfortable. I felt like I didn't belong, there were lots of good, nice people, not my kind of people. I was comfortable on the streets, in the world. So I sat there hoping nobody would notice me. They started off by giving out gifts. They were going to pull out three names out of a basket. That really made me nervous, and for the first time, I started to pray. My words were, *Please, don't let my name come up.* The first and the second names came up. I thought I had made it. Then, guess what happened. They called my name!

The program went on, and finally the speaker started to preach. He started talking about a man who came to this earth. He was God. He talked about how He undeservingly was treated so bad, how they hurt Him, whipped Him, crowned Him with thorns, spit on Him, punched Him, made Him carry a cross that was meant for three people to carry, and finally how they nailed Him to a cross. And all Jesus said was, " 'Father, forgive them, for they do not know what they are doing.' "[1]

Then I learned that He did that for me. I took it personally. I also learned that Jesus loved sinners like me and wanted to be part of my life. He accepted me just as I was and wanted to show me a better way of life. At first I couldn't believe it. I was a guy from the streets with nothing good to offer, who was dedicated to hurting others, who did drugs. I was a bad person. I had always been told that what I was doing was bad and God didn't approve of it.

I would not make it to heaven unless I changed my life. But that day, I learned that Jesus loved me so much that He gave His life for me. " 'For God so loved the world that he gave his one and only Son, that whoever believes in him shall not perish but have eternal life.' "[2] That was deep!

The preacher gave a call, inviting people to follow Jesus. I started to feel a pressure in my chest and started to get anxious. A battle started in my heart. Finally, the Holy Spirit convinced me, and I accepted Jesus as my personal Savior. I went home that night, and fell to my knees. That's when Jesus and I started our lifelong friendship.

I told Him that I wanted to follow Him, but I had many problems in my life that needed to be changed. I asked for His help with my addictions. After that moment, I have never again touched drugs or alcohol. It was quite a struggle, but somehow God did this. His power was made available to me, and He set me free from the grip of a life of misery and from the power of alcohol and drugs. A week later, I got baptized and joined God's family.

After running away from God for so long, my family and I finally found rest. Man, what had I been missing! God also offered the whole family a day of rest: the Sabbath. A day set apart to hang out with God and with each other: " 'Come to me, all you who are weary and burdened, and I will give you rest.' "[3]

I learned that God gave us the seventh day of each week as a special meeting place with Him. The Bible says it clearly: " 'Remember the Sabbath day by keeping it holy. Six days you shall labor and do all your work, but the seventh day is a Sabbath to the LORD your God. On it you shall not do any work, neither you, nor your son or daughter, nor your manservant or maidservant, nor your animals, nor the alien within your gates. For in six days the LORD made the heavens and the earth, the sea, and all that is in them, but he rested on the seventh day. Therefore the LORD blessed the Sabbath day and made it holy.' "[4]

But the most important thing I found in church was the answer I had been looking for: JESUS!

IIII—*Soldado* (Soldier)

Soon after I started my new life with Jesus, my wife and my sister Lorena followed. A whole new world opened before us as a family. Then war started. Satan was angry. I got really sick from my stomach. I went to the doctor, but they didn't find anything wrong with me. It got worse and I was in and out of the hospital. Seemed that nobody could tell me what was wrong.

Around the same time, my youngest daughter started having seizures, usually the night before church or at church. Nobody could give us answers for the cause of her problems. Then, my other daughter started having pain in her stomach. The doctors found out she had a huge tumor growing in her abdomen. I remember that everything started to break, my cars, the washer, the dryer; everything was going bad. I was barely making it.

Through it all, we kept our trust in God. I was sick for about a month, having to go to work and live a life as normal as possible, with a terrible pain in my stomach that never left. We were all pretty scared. I couldn't eat, so I lost a lot of weight. What happened next was amazing.

One day I couldn't handle the pain no more. I went outside, sat under a tree, and started to pray. As I was telling God that I couldn't go on with this problem, I was interrupted by a phone call. It was a nurse from a nearby clinic I had visited, telling me they had found what was wrong with me and had already called in my prescription. I had bacteria that were eating my stomach from the inside out. Man, was I happy they had found what it was.

We also took our daughter to a specialist for seizures, and he told us there was a chance she would never have one again. He was right. My other daughter had her tumor taken out, and after some testing, it was shown to be a benign tumor, not cancerous. Then I got a refund check in the mail saying I had overpaid on some bill, so I was able to fix everything. God is good!!! Satan lost that battle and left us alone for a while. But he would return and attack my family in the worst possible way.

It was March 29, 2007. God has blessed me with my own construction company. It was a normal day, the job we were doing that day was a hard job but it was going really well. We were pouring a concrete patio that was pretty far from home. The day before, I got home very late from work, and I didn't even see my kids. I was happy this day because we were able to finish the job early, which meant I could beat the traffic and get home earlier than usual. The whole way home I was thinking of things I would do with the kids when I got there. There was very light traffic, and it seemed even the lights would turn green as I got close to the intersections.

My kids always waited for me by the window. As soon as they saw me, they would run out to greet me with hugs and kisses. I got home. I got out of the truck, which was pulling my tractor. As soon as I saw my daughter, I knew something was terribly wrong. I saw my wife running out and screaming with a look of terror on her face. I finally realized what had happened.

One of the twins had run out first; she tried to jump on the trailer, her foot slipped, and she went under. I lay under the trailer with her for a few minutes. The next thing I remember is I looked over at my family. They were all huddled together looking at me, but I started running to the back of my house. I didn't run to them because I felt it was my fault. Then I saw a cop running over to me, we grabbed each other in a bear hug. Poor guy, I was squeezing him as tight as I could, and asking why.

I was not thinking straight, my mind was not all there. My old ways tried to surface, and I remembered my old hiding place: alcohol. The morning of the funeral, I decided that after all the people left, I would buy a case of beer, get drunk, and cry my baby in peace. I would abandon God and go back to my old ways. I went through the day in a daze, but when I woke up the next morning, I was sober! There had been a Sabbath between the accident and the funeral, and on that day, I had raised a special prayer to God. I asked for strength for the family and me. I asked for His protection, and for Him not to let me fall. Let me tell you, God is faithful!

In my confusion and pain, God gave me a special message:

"For my thoughts are not your thoughts,
    neither are your ways my ways,"
  declares the LORD.
"As the heavens are higher than the earth,
    so are my ways higher than your ways
    and my thoughts than your thoughts."[5]

I knew that my daughter was also His daughter, and if He let the accident happen, He knew why. He was also hurting and crying for my daughter along with us. I decided I would put all my trust in my Lord, and that's what my family and I did.

There will be a special reunion for our family on resurrection day. I have asked my Lord to grant me the privilege to be at Alicia's grave when she opens her eyes. When she died, she was going to greet her dad; when she awakes, I have to be there to take her in my arms.

I know that what happened to Alicia was an attack from Satan himself trying to knock me out. I claim Jesus' words to Peter when He said, " 'Simon, Simon, Satan has asked to sift you as wheat. But I have prayed for you, Simon, that your faith may not fail. And when you have turned back, strengthen your brothers.' "[6]

You too can write your name in place of Simon. You see, Satan's plan backfired, he thought he would reclaim my soul by attacking my family in order to turn me away from God, but instead, he inspired me to work harder for the cause of Christ. When Satan messes with one of God's children, he can't win. And that's because Jesus will never, ever turn His back on you. Jesus was there with me and my family, more than ever.

The way I decided to get back at the devil, the way I would get "my" punches in, is by fighting with Jesus to snatch souls from him. I recently started The Way Ministries, in the middle of the *barrio* where I grew up, to minister and try to reach ex and active gang members. God is blessing! My sister Erica and my dad—Beto—have come to the Lord. My brother Chapo, after being shot, stabbed numerous times, and hit so many times in fights, has also given his life to Jesus.

My mother is a holy woman of God who never gave up praying for us. Her family was all messed up, now we all serve the Lord and His cause. I can truly say, " 'But as for me and my household, we will serve the LORD.' "[7]

My homie or homegirl, I don't know who you are and I don't know what you are going through. But I will just tell you this: JESUS is the Way. Don't wait any longer. He is waiting for you with open arms. Jesus loves you more than anybody else in this world. You will also find rest and the answers you have been looking for in Him. That's my prayer for you.

---

1. Luke 23:34.
2. John 3:16.
3. Matthew 11:28.
4. Exodus 20:8–11.
5. Isaiah 55:8, 9.
6. Luke 22:31, 32.
7. Joshua 24:15.

The author still owns a concrete company and directs The Way Ministries, a study group for young adults, specializing in at-risk youth.

FROM A "VATO LOCO" TO A "VATO LOCO 4 JESUS"

CARLOS ACOSTA

Where are you from, *ese*? Was that the question I needed to answer that afternoon? It had been five days since my baptism. In other words, I had joined a new gang and I had "moved" into a new *barrio,* the *barrio* of Jesus Christ. It was a Wednesday afternoon in Compton, California, and I was heading up to pick up my *jefita,* at her job in my old 1975 four-door Ford Granada, when two *cholos,* or gang bangers, in another car next to me screamed, "Where're you from, *ese*?" That question was very familiar to me; I had answered it many times in the past five years, without any hesitation. I was proud of my gang and my nickname, and I was always willing to throw my gang sign and ready to put up a fist or a gun to anybody and everybody for my *barrio,* my territory. The question left me puzzled, and I honestly didn't know what to say.

"How am I going to answer these *vato*s?" I asked myself. There was a struggle inside my head. My first involuntary reaction was to answer back with my gang affiliation name, but this time it was different. "I just got baptized," I kept telling myself, "I now belong to the Jesus Christ *barrio*." Something inside me had changed and I had to be honest, so I decided to tell them the truth: "I'm from a new *barrio*," I said. "I don't gang bang no more, *ese*. I'm a Christian now; I'm from the Jesus Christ Gang."

You should have seen their faces; at first they seemed confused, but their confusion turned into rage very quickly. Quicker then I could react, they were off their car with guns in their hands. According to them, I had to be lying since not so long ago they had seen me on the streets hitting their *barrios* with drive-by shootings in my '75 Ford Granada, and I still had the demeanor of a gang member. As soon as I assessed what was taking place, and as quickly as I could, I sped up through Compton Boulevard at speeds of seventy miles per hour, passing red lights and dodging cars, praying and talking to God along the way and telling Him, "Jesus, Homeboy, help me. Now that I belong to Your *barrio,* You got to help me, Homie! I'm really trying to be good, and do the right thing, dear Jesus. Please get me out of this mess! I don't want to go back to the same life and grab my guns and my homeboys and turn against these *vatos*! I have learned now that I have to trust in You fully and that is what I'm trying to do." I kept looking at the rearview mirror as I was praying, but I could still see them coming. The praying continued: "Please help me, let them crash or something but don't let them catch me."

They didn't crash. God began to show me on that day that Jesus loved those homeboys as much as He loved me. I got away, thank God, but my poor mom had a long walk and a long bus ride home that day. After my narrow escape, I went back home where I felt safe, and stayed there the rest of the day.

It was my first big test. I was struggling inside of me. I wanted to retaliate hard, they had disrespected me, but at the same time, I had taken a new vow. I had accepted Jesus in my life and I was going to live by His Word. That meant that all my thinking and actions where now going to be according to Jesus.

Something had happened only five days earlier. The last five years of my life had been transformed. Those five days brought me freedom from addictions to rock cocaine and alcohol; freedom from all the guilt I had accumulated all those years of gang banging, drug selling, hurting others, waking up on the streets, and in and out of jail. I had found a new Homeboy, Jesus Christ, who took me as I was, who understood me, who could help me in my struggles, who could show me how to live a life free of all the troubles I had gotten myself into.

I was so thankful when I finally met Him that I decided to transfer into the Jesus Christ *barrio* and be even more faithful to Him than I was to my old *barrio*. Thinking about all that and about the way Jesus impacted my life, I decided to call my church homeboys and instead of asking them to grab their guns, we grabbed the Sword, the Word of God. Instead of retaliating, we decided to pray. I had big challenges before me, since I was still a member of a gang. Would I be allowed to walk away or not? Would they kill me or let me go? What about the rest of my enemies? Would they come back to kill me or not? One thing I knew for sure was that my Homeboy Jesus was at my side no matter what happened.

My life before I met Jesus

Growing up as a teen in Los Angeles, California, I faced the challenges that many teens face today. I was born in East Los Angeles at the General Hospital. We lived in the East L.A. projects. My *jefita* came from San Salvador, El Salvador, in the seventies and my *jefito* came from Durango, Mexico, around the same time. Both met and married in Los Angeles. I have two *carnalitas* (sisters) and one *carnal* (brother). Because of our culture mix, we called ourselves a taco-pupusa-pizza family, which are the foods representative of the three countries we have in our blood.

From East Los we moved to Korea Town near downtown L.A., and finally my *jefitos* realized the American dream of home ownership. My parents bought a house in Compton, California, where I spent the most important years of my adolescence. Out of all the places we called home, I do not recall one stress-free neighborhood; they were all in the not-so-good parts of town. Generally, we had to walk to school on streets infested with gangs, drugs, and prostitution activity. The one conclusion my friends and I quickly arrived at was, "We better stay together and protect ourselves as a group." In other words, we had to survive.

My friends and I, just like any other teenagers, had several emotional and psychological needs that needed to be met, so we began a quest to fill those needs, but only in the worst way possible. The biggest need I had as a teen was to belong. I had a desperate urge to be part of something that would give me a sense of accomplishment. I wanted to be part of something that would recognize me as a person. I wanted to be a part of something that would value my thoughts, my efforts. I wanted to be a part of something where I would be appreciated and loved.

For me, it all started in the seventh grade. When I first walked the school yard at Berendo Jr. High School in Los Angeles, it was very scary. I quickly noticed almost everyone being a part of a group. There were the skaters in one corner, the punk rockers on another corner. We had the break dancers, the rappers, the gang bangers, and all of a sudden it dawned on me: *What about me? Where do I belong?* To make matters worse, I had no friends. I knew not one. The pressure started that same day. "Look at his tight pants!" "Look at his pretty shirt!" "Do you still let your mommy dress you?" The worst thing is that their criticism rang true. My clothes were totally out of place. My Payless shoes didn't help, either. I started to pressure my parents into buying the clothes and the shoes the rest of the kids were wearing, the kind that would allow me to get lost in the crowd. But even after the wardrobe makeover, I still had a question to answer: Where did I belong? Was it with the *paisas,* the rockers, the Mexicans, the Salvadorians, the skaters, the gangsters …?

In a very strange way, as I was going through all this, my family and I were regular members of a church, and for the most part, I considered myself a Christian, but to my disadvantage, I began to build stronger ties with the gang than with my Christian friends and values. It was there, in the gang, that my need for belonging was met.

"If you want to be part of this gang, holmes," I was told, "you're in it forever," they said. "You will have to live by its code, you will have to dress like we dress, and you will also defend it anywhere you go." I decided to join.

But before it became official, I had to fight two gang members for thirteen seconds. I did. Those were the slowest thirteen seconds of my entire life. By the end of those thirteen seconds, I was hurt. I was bleeding from my lips, and my left eye was bruised. My whole body hurt. That was my "baptism" into the gang. I got my nickname and all the gang members came and hugged me. They said, "You are part of *la familia* now." "You will be part of this gang forever, *ese.*" "*Somos pocos pero locos.*" "*Por vida, ese*" (for life). And that was the beginning of a journey that brought my family and me a lot of sadness and pain for almost five years.

I began to wear pants size 40, when my waist measured no more then 28 inches; and they had to be Dickies. We made so much money for that company! I shaved my head and decided to get tattoos on the back and front of my arms. I now had a mission, to defend my *barrio,* even to the point of death.

Being new in a gang brings a lot of pressure, since you have to prove to others that you're worthy of being part of the family/gang. Stealing and going after the enemies of the gang became my way of earning respect among my peers. Soon, I found myself in the highest ranks of the gang. I was part of something pretty big and that made me feel very important, in a weird way. For a little while, I felt a certain kind of contentment and security, but in the end, all it really brought was discomfort and sadness for me and my family.

In the tenth grade, I dropped out of high school and started experimenting with marijuana and rapidly escalating to a very addictive drug called cocaine. I also became "a regular" at the local jail. My first arrest was for possession of a loaded firearm. At another time, I was arrested after committing an armed robbery with a deadly weapon. Some of my homies and I were taken to Eastlake Juvenile Hall in East Los Angeles, California. I spent that night in a dark cell. There, making sure that no one listened, I began to cry.

God has a strange way of showing up at the lowest end, the most lonely places, of our lives, so I began to remember God in there. I asked myself, *What happened with all the happiness I found in the gang? What have I done with my life?*

The next day, my *jefitos* came to visit me in jail. It was very hard for my parents to see me in a prison suit. It was hard especially for my mother. With tears in her eyes, she reminded me of how she and Dad had dedicated me to the Lord at church. With tears in their eyes, they pointed to the building next door, the General Hospital where I was born. They specifically pointed to the hospital floor where seventeen years ago, I had been born. I thought to myself, *How can life change so tragically?* I also thought of the irony of being across the street from a maternity ward. In one building there was life and dreams of a great life with no limits, in the other building there was death and shattered dreams.

So, here I was now, in Juvenile Hall, waiting for a trial with two heartbroken parents. But I learned that they were heartbroken but never defeated. They took me by my hands, knelt, and prayed. They plead to God for mercy and for another chance, they asked Him not to abandon me, and the Lord heard their prayers on that very day.

It amazes me now how the human heart can be so deceiving. I had prayed with my parents for God to help me, but as soon as I got out of jail, I went back to my old ways, which made things even worse for me and my family. But something else began to unfold before me. It seemed like one by one, a lot of my friends began to die, most of them victims of the rival gangs. I witnessed the death of a friend called "Silent," and then came the turns for "Spooky," "Ghost," "Smiley," and many others who lost their valuable lives protecting a territory that wasn't even ours. Every funeral took a part of me, for they were a constant reminder that death was knocking on the door. But after every funeral, our rivals had to plan another funeral, since retaliation became our way of mourning. We felt a strange moral obligation to respond to the killing of our friends, and revenge was the only way. Looking back, I wonder why I wasn't able to see the vicious cycle we were all trapped in, as if killing someone would bring back the lost.

Meeting Jesus all over again

Just the thought of what took place that night gives me the chills. It happened on a Friday. "Joker" and I were the "lookout" soldiers for the night. It was our job to take care of the *barrio*. I would stand at the corner of the street we were to protect and my friend would stand exactly halfway between me and the other corner of the block. My job was to spot any suspicious cars or individuals who were our enemies. Standing on a corner late that Friday night, a car approached me and asked me if I sold drugs. I told them I didn't, but I could point him in the right direction towards my friend, the drug dealer.

Soon after, the deal was taking place in the middle of the street, but when my friend handed the buyer the drugs, he tried to get away without paying. My friend quickly pulled out a baseball bat and began to hit the guy, who was still in his car, but somehow he managed to get away. He was beaten so badly that he ended up crashing his car a block away from us. We thought he had died.

It was almost 3:00 A.M., so we decided to call it off and go home. As I walked towards my house, I remember thinking my parents and brothers would soon be getting ready to go to church. I also remembered that my mother had invited me to join them. Earlier that night, before I left the house, my mother had invited me to sing and to pray with them, but I was way too busy to waste my time with God. Besides, I knew they constantly prayed for me in my rebellion. The reason I knew this was that on many occasions there were bullets shot at me that ended elsewhere, and it just seemed like every time death was near, there was always a certain special protection I could never explain. I know now it was due to the prayers of my mother and father. God seems to have a special place in His heart for a parent's prayer, and I know that His protection over me was His way of honoring my parents' faith. God was not going to let go of me, even when I had no love for Him.

I slept for a few short hours and around 7:00 A.M., one of my gang-banger friends knocked on my window. "Come over, *carnal,* the enemies have just killed four of our homeboys." I got up as quickly as I could and went to see what had happened.

An old familiar scene, the same *vato* who tried to steal the drugs came back and took revenge. He killed four of my friends that morning. As I stood there, I watched how their mothers would hug their lifeless bodies crying to God to bring them back to life. The image of a mother being stained by the blood of her child and crying uncontrollably was too much for me. At that moment, I heard the voice of God telling me: *"Carlos, it's time. Stop running from Me. This is the way you will end up if you keep on running from Me. Come back to Me, Carlos."* God was calling me. He had not given up on me all those years. And without knowing, my life was about to be transformed completely. It would be a 180-degree turn, and it was all for the better.

I went home that morning and found that my parents had gone to church. In my sadness, I started to use crystal meth. I found myself overdosing that morning. My heart was palpitating, my vision was blurry, and I began to shake. I kept taking more and more, but even the drugs were completely useless this time.

I felt lonely and very scared. I took a hard look at my life and my very few accomplishments. I was nineteen years old and I had seen much more than normal people see in their entire lives. What kind of life was this? I had dropped out of school, had been in and out of jail, and was addicted to drugs. Someone was always trying to kill me, I couldn't keep a job, et cetera. I began to feel depressed to the point that I decided to take my own life and end my pain and misery right there.

But as I was playing with the idea of suicide, I remembered my parents. I remembered their prayers and the many times they had told me about a God with a plan for my life. I began to wonder if all of that was true, and the possibility of an all loving God, sort of like my parents, who would never give up on me. I don't know at what moment the suicidal thoughts disappeared, but all of a sudden, I saw myself praying out loud with a Bible in my hands: "God, please, please help me. I give up, Lord. I want to stop running from You. I have lost my way in this life. I made the wrong decisions, Lord. I'm so lonely, so afraid, and so sad. Here I am, Lord. Forgive me. Please accept me as I am."

I don't even know when, but after a long time of praying and crying, I ended up falling asleep. I slept so much that when my parents came back late that Sabbath afternoon, they came to my room to wake me up. I was so happy to see them.

The next day my parents invited me to an evangelistic crusade. For the first time in almost ten years, I finally accepted an invitation to go to church. I sat there and listened to the preacher talk about Jesus Christ. From the perspective of a gang member, Jesus became very attractive to me. I heard how He came to die for all of us in this world. How He left His *barrio* (heaven) to come to our *barrio* (earth) and how He also formed a gang of twelve disciples whom He trained to talk and live for the mission of the gang.

There were a lot of similarities with my gang. The thing that impacted me the most was learning that Jesus, the Leader of this gang, died on a cross to free people like me from the power of the devil; that by His death I could receive a new life free of drugs, misery, and pain. As a gang member, I was attracted to Jesus even more after knowing that He had beaten death forever. I was very impressed. So when the preacher made a special call to accept the new life that Jesus gives, I stood up and walked. There I was like the prodigal son, walking towards the altar with size 40 pants, addicted to drugs, bald headed, arms full of tattoos. I fell on my knees and asked God to forgive me while at the same time accepting the gift of Jesus Christ.

Life after meeting Jesus

I got baptized on October 1994 at the Central Spanish Seventh-day Adventist Church in Los Angeles. This baptism was different. I wasn't going to fight anyone for thirteen seconds. This time I was going to make a new oath, an oath with God. I was deciding to live a life in Jesus Christ. I was going to be part of a new *barrio,* His church. That Saturday morning, my parents were there and were crying once again. But this time, their tears were of joy and happiness. My mother was screaming so loud, "This is my son, God has returned him to us, and He has answered our prayers!" There in the water, my parents and I hugged for a long time. "Welcome home, *mijo,*" they said. "Welcome home, *mijo.*"

*****

Life was different now. I was experiencing a complete change. My thoughts were different. My desires were different. I did not need drugs or to hurt others to feel appreciated or significant. Now, all I needed was my Homeboy Jesus, who gave me, and continues to give me, happiness. A new person was born that day. New clothes, new thoughts, new desires.

Please, do not misunderstand, there were very many challenges still ahead, but I knew Jesus was not going to let me down. One of my first challenges was figuring out how to tell my *barrio* boys that

I no longer wanted to be part of them. I remembered the oath I took when I joined the gang—that I would never get out of it, only through death. Still, I decided to face them. When I arrived at the park where my gang used to hang out, I told them how I had become a Christian and that I no longer was going to be part of the gang. Many laughed at me, others were angry; one of them hit me on my face. They said, "Come back tomorrow, maybe you will have changed your mind." I left that day crying and sad, but I had made a promise to God. I had promised Him that I would share Jesus with my gang and my enemies.

I went back to my gang and preached to them. Many listened to me. They said that I could not get out of the gang, but instead they wanted me to help them find a better way. They made me agree to keep visiting them and their families, especially when they had difficult times. Until today, I continue to visit and write to them in prison. I have shared with them the love of Christ. Many have become Christians behind prison walls, and sadly, many others have been killed.

One year later, in 1995, I got my GED. In 1996, I went to college in Mexico to become a pastor. I graduated in 2000. That same year, I was assigned my first pastoral duty as a chaplain in southern Mexico. Also that very same year, the Lord blessed me with a wonderful wife, Alma. In 2001, I was given a scholarship to study a master's degree in Family Relations, and graduated from it in 2003. From 2003 to 2005, God gave me the opportunity to work as a marriage/family and drug addiction counselor in the State of Colorado. In 2005, I worked as an intern at the World Headquarters of the Seventh-day Adventist Church, located in Silver Spring, Maryland. Then a wonderful blessing came, our children: Karla-Michelle and Emily. Since 2006, I have been working as a youth pastor in my *barrio*, Los Angeles.

How sweet it has been to live with a true Homeboy like Jesus Christ! It's now been fourteen years since I moved into a new *barrio* with Jesus. Since my baptism and for every day of those fourteen years, I have been living a wonderful journey with Him.

I pray that He can also become your Homeboy. Be a part of His *barrio* today. Let Him give you a new life that you never imagined you could have.

Carlos Acosta is the youth pastor of the Hollywood Spanish Seventh-day Adventist Church in Los Angeles, California.

Carlos Acosta before:

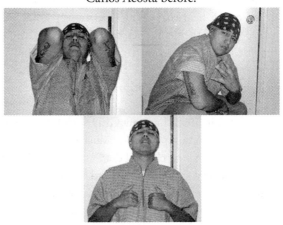

nothing for you on the other side? It is a horrible realization knowing that you are a failure.

I thought about many things that night. You see, my wife had left me. We had been married for three years. I was devastated, I truly loved her. We got married while she was still in high school. We met in the beautiful city of Miami. We had a lot in common. She was the one God had chosen for me, we were born for each other. However, I had a personal demon and did not know it, one who hates to see me happy, who is always leading me astray. He wants my failure. He knows how to mess up a life, my life and yours.

Trash

My story, my pain, goes back to the eighties. I was born in Nicaragua. A very hostile country back then, I saw my share of death and blood. I was acquainted with the reality that we live in a very inhospitable world from an early age. They called it *"la revolución"* (the revolution). These were turbulent times for my family. We were forced to leave. I can never forget crossing "the Jordan River" into "the Promised Land." I mean, el Río Grande. That's right, I am a wetback. The journey led me to Miami, the place where I grew up, the place that I now called home. I thought the war was behind me. Who would have known that I had come to fight a battle of my own in the land of the free?

Like many of the Latinos in this country, I was brought up in a dysfunctional family. My dad was a good man, but he was an alcoholic. The adjusting years were difficult. I was a troubled teen growing up in a gang infested Little Havana. I learned the ways of the streets early on. I had no choice. I avoided the gang lifestyle but couldn't avoid the other trash that the world offered. Yes, it is trash. Now I know that it makes you feel filthy and worthless.

Numb

I tried alcohol for the first time when I was about fourteen years old. Just an "innocent" taste. That's all it took, I was hooked. That *probadita* took me into a ten-year journey in numbness and dumbness. I became an addict. During my party years, I tried different drugs, but still my drug of preference was alcohol. The demon of alcohol was fighting for my heart and I did not realize it. I went through that stage of my life like a zombie. The devil knows how important the teenage years are. Important decisions are made, we have more energy and our passions develop. It is not by coincidence that the Bible describes amazing stories of young men and women who did extraordinary things in the hands of God, and yet I find myself back in that dark room.

I looked around and I saw my house destroyed. I don't remember to this day what happened. I just know that I was drunk to the point of insanity, and I destroyed my house and mistreated my wife. Luckily, the pain I inflicted wasn't physical, yet I can't imagine the emotional pain hurting less. I was possessed by a demon, is how I explain it, and I probably was. Grace is weird, in the midst of this chaos, the confusion and pain, I realized that I was not alone. In the midst of it all, I knew that Someone loved me. In the midst of my drunkenness, I knew that God' grace was sufficient for me. I closed my eyes and drifted away to a humble room in the church of my childhood. I remembered the stories of Sabbath School that gave me hope, that made me want to live. I grew up as a Seventh-day Adventist, until the demons of alcohol robbed me of my teenage years.

Love

Like water to the thirsty, I longed for the reassurance of God's presence. I wondered if it was possible for God to mend the shattered pieces of my life. Was He so merciful that He would accept someone like me? I doubted He would. However, God's ways are not my ways. That's why I learned to love God. His love is persistent, consistent, and insistent. He does not take no for an answer because God is love. God falls head over heels for us. It was on that very sad day, at the bottom of a bottle, that God began His mysterious plan for me.

Many things happened that are too gruesome to share. Needless to say, I did not conquer my demons in one shot; I fell a few more times. I made bad decisions, fell into big trouble, and had emptiness inside me. Like the Israelites of old, I kept messing up and giving up, until I grew tired and surrendered my life to Christ.

Maybe you can relate to my story. Maybe you find yourself fighting your own demons, wishing life would just end, you are so tired of living. Don't end it, hold on, God will find a way. I know God will; He found one for me. I made it through; I am alive because I chose to surrender, to literally give up fighting my own demons and fall on the Rock, Jesus Christ. That decision gave me life and freedom in Jesus. After my surrender to Jesus, He gave me the strength to revolt against the enemy and fight back.

We are called to fight, but not in our strength, because the battle belongs to the Lord. I rose up in His arms and His grace sustained me. I picked up my sword and He gave me His Spirit. I put on His armor and He gave me His victory. We went out to fight, and I have never looked back.

Fourth of July

This is a special holiday for U.S. citizens. It celebrates the adoption of the Declaration of Independence on July 4, 1776, signaling freedom from Great Britain. This is a day that I also celebrate for very different reasons. I celebrate having been in jail. Don't laugh. It is an important day for me.

Let me share my Fourth of July experience with you. I was locked up, but I found freedom. The jail in Key West reminded me of my condition. I saw myself enslaved by sin and locked up by the devil. Like the Midianites of old, the devil was my foe. My soul was restless, I was not happy. I had tried the world and was left unsatisfied. It was draining me, robbing me, and killing me. However, I am glad that Jesus fights for my heart. It was inside that jail that I gave up and surrendered to Christ. There I made the decision to follow Him.

There has been no turning back. I have never gotten drunk again. I am out of my hiding place, out of the darkness, and into His marvelous light. I am out fighting for His glory. It has been a wild adventure. We started seeking for God in the Miami Central Church, a Seventh-day Adventist church in Little Havana, Miami. It was a struggle, but I was free—free to live, free at last. I had met Jesus. Now I was headed in another direction.

Jesus has given me security through His love, meaning through His life, and hope to live for. I ended up with His Word in my hands and His Spirit in my heart. I was lost but now I was found. By the way, in case you are wondering, my wife did come back and we have been happily married for fourteen years. We are blessed with two beautiful daughters.

Revolution

You see, in order for the Israelites to be free, they had to trust in God and revolt. They had to stand up against their enemies. Hiding in caves would not accomplish anything. Revolution means to turn around. The word has a negative connotation to it; we may think of Fidel Castro or Chavez when we hear it, but it is not a bad word. It is a good word. The Israelites needed to revolt. We are called to be part of a revolution which has already begun. It began thousands of years ago, Jesus started it, and it is marked by His blood. Mark Twain said, "No people in this world ever did achieve their freedom by goody-goody talk and moral suasion: *it being an immutable law that all revolutions that will succeed, must begin in blood.*" This revolution will succeed. It also began with blood, but Jesus defeated death and He will come back soon!

Another fact about a revolution is that it begins in the mind of a revolutionary. Ralph Waldo Emerson said, "*Every revolution was first a thought in one man's mind,* and when the same thought occurs in another man, it is the key to that era." A turnaround of things that just aren't right begins in one's mind. In the heart of who we are. A revolutionary is not happy with the ways things are, for us it may mean the way we are living our lives. That's why Paul says, "Set your minds on things above, not on earthly things."[4] It all begins in your mind, your heart. You feel you must live out your convictions. You must allow God to transform your mind, so He can stir a revolution in you.

Revolt

The story of the Israelites goes on to say that a revolt was started. It was initiated by God. They cried out to the Lord.[5] The first thing that God did was to stir the heart of a revolutionary. Notice that a revolutionary does not need to have a great pedigree. God chose a farmer that was also afraid of the Midianites. However, God knew what he could become in His hands. I like the way the Lord greeted him: " 'Mighty hero, the LORD is with you!' "[6] A hero? But he is in hiding! Please notice the first reaction of this "hero": " 'But sir,' Gideon replied, 'if the LORD is with us, why has all this happened to us? Where are all his wonders that our fathers told us about?' "[7] He complains. The Lord gives him a shocking answer: " 'Go in the strength you have and save Israel out of Midian's hand. Am I not sending you?' "[8] In other words, God saw beyond his flaws, and invited Gideon to trust Him and experience what He can do.

This invitation is given to all of us. God has a unique call for each of us. It is a call to an adventure, to the unknown, to an exciting lifestyle, a life of faith. We are called to live a raw and undomesticated life of faith. Are you ready to accept living this dangerous lifestyle? Gideon succumbed to the human tendency to look at himself: " 'But Lord,' Gideon asked, 'how can I save Israel? My clan is the weakest in Manasseh, and I am the least in my family.' "[9] He didn't get it and he did at the same time. God plainly told him that he was going to rescue Israel by His power. Gideon also recognized his limitations. This is a great lesson for us. We need to be humble enough to accept the fact that we cannot do it on our own and to accept the promise that God will fight for us. We are called to revolt against the enemy by being in the army of God, to allow Michael to lead us into battle and to accept his call to the post that He has assigned for us.

Called

I had been in the church for about a year when I realized that the Lord was calling me to be a minister. "Me, a pastor? No way, Lord, I am the weakest of my clan. I am introverted, I can't talk well, I am not a scholar, I have many flaws. I am too short, the list is too long. Are You sure, Lord? Maybe You got the wrong person." God's reply was, " 'My grace is sufficient for you, for my power is made perfect in weakness.' "[10]

I have to admit that I was not convinced, and I had to ask God for many signs, like Gideon did. God came through each time. He saw something in me that He could use for His glory.

There is nothing more fulfilling than doing what God has called you to do in life. That is why it is vital to place your life in God's hands early on in life. He will lead you to the right career path. He will lead you to the right person. Most importantly, He will assign you to the right post so you can fight for His kingdom. Is there any practical way of finding God's unique calling for your life? The following guidelines will help you figure it out: pray, learn (read the Bible and other resources), begin with what you enjoy, experiment as much as possible, check your effectiveness, and ask the opinion of others.[11] Give it a try, it is worth it. I now live to preach the good news of Jesus Christ, and I experience His power often. I have seen it. I have seen demons flee from His presence. I have seen lives transformed. Jesus gives you the life you always wanted! May you accept the call to fight for the heart of your King. Remember, He fights for yours!

The Spirit

This is a spiritual war. I found this out when I was in a room rebuking demons that had taken over the life of a teenager. Several demons had possessed his heart. I found out that we are not equipped to fight the enemy. We cannot fight temptations on our own. We can only fight back if God is with us. Gideon was on the same boat. He could not defeat over 135,000 men on his own. The story says, "Then the Spirit of the Lord came upon Gideon, and he blew a trumpet, summoning the Abiezrites to follow him."[12] The courage to take up arms against the principalities comes from God. He will stir our souls until we rise up and stand for Jesus. We are called to blow the "horn" of salvation to those who are lost and empty.

There is an army of young people in our church led by the Holy Spirit that are rising against the world. There is an old prophecy that is being fulfilled:

"And afterward,
    I will pour out my Spirit on all people.
Your sons and daughters will prophesy,
    your old men will dream dreams,
    your young men will see visions."[13]

Do you want to be part of this movement?

Fallen

I am lucky to be alive. Many of my friends and even family were not as lucky. In a recent trip to Nampa, Idaho, a survivor from the gang lifestyle took me to different places in the *barrio* were many of his friends had been killed. It reminded me again that the battle is real. It also reminded me of the fallen that I have known. Even in my own family, there's a cousin serving thirty years in a federal prison. A friend is struggling with crack addiction. I could go on and on. I bet you have your own list. The fallen. People that haven't made it yet. There are many who want out. They can make it out if you blow the horn of salvation. Will you?

The three hundred

In 480 B.C., a small force of three hundred Spartans and eleven hundred Thespians and Thebans led by King Leonidas made a legendary last stand at the Battle of Thermopylae against the massive Persian army (over three hundred thousand), inflicting a very high casualty rate on the Persian forces before finally being encircled.[14] This story might sound familiar, it is the movie *300*.

The story of Gideon that I have been referring to is very similar. Gideon gathered his troops, about thirty-two thousand answered to the call but not all were eager to fight. God knew this and found a way to sift them out. Gideon told his troops, " ' "Anyone who trembles with fear may turn back and leave Mount Gilead." ' "[15] So twenty-two thousand men left, while ten thousand remained. But the Lord saw that there were still too many, and He gave Gideon further instructions.

Gideon took the men down to the water. And the Lord told him, " 'Separate those who lap the water with their tongues like a dog from those who kneel down to drink.' Three hundred men lapped with their hands to their mouths. All the rest got down on their knees to drink. The LORD said to Gideon, 'With the three hundred men that lapped I will save you and give the Midianites into your hands. Let all the other men go, each to his own place.' "[16] You see, those who were eager to fight were those who scooped out the water with their hands and kept on marching, but those who were afraid were buying time, they were delaying their duty.

This is the story of the three hundred chosen by God to fight and bring about victory. I think you are one of those! God is calling you to fight. He has chosen you to be part of the three hundred through whom He will bring victory. God has a plan. It includes you! He sees in you a "mighty hero" in His hands. Are you going to respond? It is my hope that you may embrace God's calling today. May you hear His voice calling you to fight. May you revolt against the world by standing for Jesus. May you fight for the heart of your King, for He fights for yours!

1. Adapted from Erwin McManus, *The Barbarian Way* (Nashville, Tenn.: Thomas Nelson, Inc., 2005).

2. Revelation 12:7–12.

3. 1 Timothy 6:12.

4. Colossians 3:2.

5. Judges 6:7.

6. Verse 12, NLT.

7. Verse 13.

8. Verse 14.

9. Verse 15.

10. 2 Corinthians 12:9.

11. Christian Schwarz, *The 3 Colors of Ministry* (Ill.: ChurchSmart Resources, 2001), 55–63.

12. Judges 6:34.

13. Joel 2:28.

14. Peter Green, *The Greco-Persian Wars* (Berkeley and Los Angeles, Calif.: University of California Press, 1998),140.

15. Judges 7:3.

16. Verses 5–7.

Harold Altamirano is a youth pastor in the Oregon Conference. He is a frequent speaker and evangelist to the English-speaking Hispanic youth.

ANSWERING THE CALL: A JOURNEY OF FAITH

YAMI BAZÁN

I'm not sure if you can relate with me ... but, have you ever heard a powerful speaker preach just a phenomenal sermon about how God has completely turned their life around and got them out of drugs, alcohol, or just a really messy situation, and all you could do as the listener is nod your head and think, *Wow!* But really deep inside you were thinking, *Man, I'm sure it is easy to totally serve God when you have had THAT experience ... but I've never done any of that and by the way, I'm not planning on it either.*

You see, that was my predicament all through high school and college. I sat through hundreds (yeah, you read right!) of Week of Prayers because I was what they called a "PK," or a pastor's kid, which means I basically lived at church not just on Sabbaths like most Adventists, but also Sundays for Pathfinders, Wednesdays for prayer meetings, Friday nights for Vespers, and every other day for whatever other office I had been nominated to lead. That happens a lot to PKs. We are given all sorts of responsibilities, just because; like the one time I was nominated to be the pianist for my Sabbath School. The problem: I did not play the piano.

The bottom line is that I always longed to have a conversion story of sorts. I wanted to share how God had completely changed me and had turned my life around. But in reality, God was an integral part of my life and of my story. I did not know life without

Him. I had not experienced life without Him. And I didn't want to either. I knew that He was my everything. My core. He was the goodness that I knew surrounded me. Yet at times, I must admit, I almost was jealous of those who had wandered away and had come back with a story of their own.

Does it remind you of a biblical character? A brother, to be exact? The story of the prodigal son is often told to remind us of the love the Father has for each and every single one of us, and His excitement when we decide to come back home. Yet the story also has a second character, a brother. You find the story in Luke 15:11–31. But you encounter this second brother towards the end of the story in verses 28–30: " 'The older brother became angry and refused to go in. So his father went out and pleaded with him. But he answered his father, "Look! All these years I've been slaving for you and never disobeyed your orders. Yet you never gave me even a young goat so I could celebrate with my friends. But when this son of yours who has squandered your property with prostitutes comes home, you kill the fattened calf for him!" ' "

In a sense, my sentiments were a bit different. I didn't mind the celebration and the welcome home of those who had left. I just minded that somehow I did not have such an exciting story to tell. And in reality, I didn't have a grasp on God like they did. Though I had stayed "home" and served God faithfully, it seemed as if they somehow felt a closeness to God that surpassed anything I had felt before. It seemed as if God revealed Himself in the past through the prophets and in the present through the prodigal sons and daughters who had left home. And I was neither of those cases. Yet I wanted God to reveal Himself to me.

I started to become dissatisfied with my journey. I couldn't see myself leaving God or the church. Here were my mentors—teachers, friends, family—and I knew that to run away would never bring me the peace my soul seemed to be longing for. Instead I began to pray. This wasn't a "happy" prayer. This was really a very frustrated prayer. By now I was in my twenties and it seemed that I was losing my spiritual joy more and more, and a sense of routine had taken over my spiritual walk. My discontent became such, that I finally made a pact with God.

The beginning ...

Now you might wonder, *Why would anyone think they can make a pact with God? How disrespectful!* But in reality, it was a desperate conversation that went something like this: "God, I'm at the end of my spiritual rope. I'm sick of sitting in the pew every Sabbath and listening to the same sermons and nothing in my life changing. I've become a professional pew warmer and I am tired of holding down the fort. I will give You one more year of my life. If You can't transform it and me somehow, I'm done with religion, with the church, and with You."

I was smart enough to know that when you make a pact, something is required of you as well. I needed to make sure that I could set God up to succeed. Otherwise, I would always wonder, *Did I do enough?* So I told God, "I will dedicate on a daily basis two to three hours to reading Your Word and searching for answers." Now you have to understand that during this time in my life, I had recently gotten married and I was already working full time as a teacher. So that left me with very little time in the day to actually pull my end of the bargain. And of course, being newly married, I did not want to do this alone. So on a Sunday evening, I informed my husband that I would be putting the TV in the closet for a year, and I would be dedicating all that TV time to God in order to see if He was really real or not.

Danny (my very smart husband) decided not only that he would not get in the way of his determined wife but more importantly, that he would join me on this quest. And so it began. I wish I could put on paper the details of the painful and slow beginning. The awkwardness of sitting down and attempting to "feel" God for ninety minutes! It was actually quite funny. I remember Danny and I just sitting down in our living room right after dinner and opening the Bible and not knowing even where to start. So I just randomly chose a text, read it, and then we attempted to get some meaning from it. The whole experience felt pushed, fake, and almost desperate. But I had made a promise to God, and I intended on keeping it.

By the end of the first week, we had bought some Christian CDs, books, and devotionals to help us fill in the time. Slowly we noticed ourselves looking forward to this time in the evening whereby we would just pause and listen to God, each other, and the wise words of writers and musicians. I kid you not! By the third month, we knew that something had changed inside of us.

I can't really explain what had happened, it was as if scales had been removed from our eyes and the world around us just seemed different somehow. It was as if by listening to God's words, our lives had taken a different direction, focus, and energy. My job hadn't changed, my responsibilities at church had not changed, my family hadn't changed, but I had changed. People began to matter more and more, day after day. I would notice the desperate mother driving next to me with tears in her eyes. The elderly gentleman who wandered through the grocery store with sadness in his eyes that almost took my breath away. The neighbor kid next door, who just sat quietly outside while his house almost shook from all the yelling and screaming happening inside. The list goes on and on. It was as if God was waking me up from a deep sleep and reminding me that although I was "home" like the older brother, that did not mean that all was well and that there wasn't a job to do.

A leap of faith ...

That year changed me! Spiritually, I realized that I was not the older brother who had stayed home, but rather, I was the one who had left. I began to recognize in reading God's Word how far I had

CHANGED

been from His will. I began to hear in His words the calling He had given me. I held on to Jeremiah 1:4, 5: " 'Before I formed you in the womb I *knew you,* / before you were born *I set you apart'* " (emphasis supplied).

Slowly God began to open doors in my community that allowed me to explore His calling. I spoke in various chapels of nearby academies. I shared my journey at various Sabbath Schools. I began to meet with high school students and just listen to their struggles, and volunteered as a mentor at the homeless shelter. All along we kept our daily dates with God. He continued to shape our thinking and our lives in ways we never would have imagined.

And then it happened. I woke up one night around 3:00 A.M. and began to quickly write a project proposal. I wrote nonstop for almost three hours. When Danny awoke that morning, I shared with him my plan, God's Road Rules: a road trip ministry for young people. Our motto: *Save the Human Race. Share Christ.* We would travel all through the United States as missionaries to our academies, and we would share with young people our journey and remind them of their calling. We would travel in an RV (which we didn't own), and we would spend one week in each school doing a Week of Prayer, having open forums in classrooms, mentoring and counseling at night, and speaking at the local church on Sabbath. We would create a Web site and the students could follow our journey via the Web. We would become modern-day disciples: radical followers of Christ.

Needless to say, Danny was not convinced ... so for the next three months, God had to reveal to him, via all kinds of signs, that this was exactly what He envisioned for us. By June of 1998, we had sold all of our belongings, had quit our jobs, and bought an RV. I spent all summer calling the academies and creating a route. Danny finished up his job and took out our savings, and by September, we left our family and friends in Southern California and embarked on the road trip that would forever change our lives.

• 48 •

The road trip …

The idea was simple enough. We would arrive at the academy, park our RV, hook up to their water and electricity, and spend a week living life with that community. We were completely at the mercy of the guest community. Our meals would be provided by the academy and our gas would be paid by selling our God's Road Rules T-shirts, which had been donated by La Sierra University. If we needed to go to the store, we had brought our bikes, and we would pedal our way to the nearest market. We were totally dependent on God. It was an unforgettable thrill ride. I've never felt more assured, more connected, and yet so vulnerable.

In retrospect, it is a good thing that God doesn't let us see the future. If I had seen all the challenges that we were going to face, I would have been so terrified I would have never left my home. Seriously, I've never been so afraid, so lost, so alone, and so confused. I've never felt so inadequate and yet so convinced. OK, enough adjectives. Let me just share with you a couple of God-stories. Our trip was filled with these kinds of stories. Moments in which we saw the power and intervention of God so vividly, it seemed as something the Israelites would have experienced. It was so cool!

T-shirts: I told you that the T-shirts paid for our gas. Yet, how God chose to do this completely surprised us. We traveled to twenty-two academies in fourteen states, but by the fourth academy we noticed a trend. Each shirt was ten dollars, so if we sold ten shirts equivalent to one hundred dollars, that was the amount of money we could count on to arrive to the next location. The bizarre part was that time and time again, we would only sell exactly the amount of T-shirts that we would need in order to get to our next destination. Can you imagine God doing this week after week? Every single time we were completely caught off-guard. Nine months on the road, every week in a different location, and every week we would be able to see God's hand in action. It was what Danny and I labeled our twenty-first-century "manna" moments.

As if that was not enough, once I completely forgot to make the announcement in the classes, and it was Friday and we had yet to sell any shirts. We would be leaving on Sabbath, and I never sold anything on Sabbath. We were at Campion Academy in Colorado and our next destination would be Chisholm Trail Academy in Texas. We figured we would need at least $120. Danny noticed this on Thursday evening, and I did not have any more classes on Friday. In the back of my mind I wondered how God was going to fix this one.

The next morning at breakfast, an elderly gentleman approached our table. He seemed really nice. He introduced himself and then proceeded to tell us that he was a colporteur in that area and that earlier that morning, as he was talking to God, he was advised to stop by and give us some money. He handed us a fifty-dollar bill. We were shocked! He prayed for us and with us and then turned around and walked away. Danny and I just smiled. God was starting something. We could feel it. The Bible teacher who was sitting with us at breakfast asked us what we would use the money for, and we explained how we had forgotten to mention the T-shirts and that this money would be used for gas. The teacher quickly told us he would buy some shirts for his family members, and we rejoiced at how God managed to fix our problem ... but He was not done.

About three quarters of the way to Texas, we realized we were going to be short on gas. We had been driving through a terrible snowstorm, rainstorm, and dust storm and our gas gauge was on empty. We prayed about it, but did not worry too much. After all, God had provided for us just a few hours before.

Suddenly, out of nowhere, there was a huge semi behind us that began to flash its lights and honk at us. Danny checked to make sure he was in the right lane and he had no emergency lights on.

Yet the driver continued making the signals. Danny let him pass by and as the driver passed us by, he enthusiastically gave us a thumbs-up and several more honks. Evidently, he was impressed by the lettering on the side of our RV. We smiled politely and thanked him, but he continued to signal. When the next exit came up, we decided to get off and get some gas, and we noticed the truck driver getting off as well and following us to the location. Before we could even park the RV and get off, the driver was knocking at our door.

The next hour found us sitting and listening as a brand-new child of God shared his story with us. He was excited and could hardly contain himself. He left out no details. He spoke and we listened. We shared with him a bit of our journey and we prayed with him. As he was leaving, he turned around, reached for his wallet (we had NOT mentioned we needed any money), and he gave us a ten-dollar bill. He apologized for not having more. We cried because we realized that God had sent us an angel and had kept to His plan.

Tornadoes at noon: It was a Sabbath afternoon and we had left Ozark Academy in Arkansas in a hurry due to a potential snowstorm heading our way. We were scheduled to arrive at Bass Memorial Academy in Mississippi on Sunday afternoon. Danny and I were driving our RV listening to a sermon on tape and praising God for the ways He had revealed Himself at Ozark. It took a while before we realized that the two-way lane we were driving was completely deserted. There had not been a single person on the road for over an hour. We found this kind of odd because it was a little past noon and there were plenty of businesses all around us, though not a person was in sight.

Danny suggested we turn on the radio and see if we could find a local channel. Sure enough, instantly we found a station with one of those emergency notices. Usually, those types of emergency warning systems always begin with, "This is a test of the emergency broadcasting system. This is only a test. *Beeeeeeep.*" Well this one did not say anything about a test. Instead it said, "This is the emergency broadcasting system. Alert! Tornado warning for Elizabeth County residents. Again, this is NOT a test."

Danny and I looked at each other and then looked up ahead to see if we could find some type of sign, and we noticed a green sign coming up. We eagerly awaited and to our horror it read, "Welcome to Elizabeth County." I slowly looked to my right and there in the far distance was a well-formed tornado. My heart began to beat faster than I had ever experienced. I looked over at Danny to tell him what I had just seen, when I noticed that past him, to my left, was another fully formed tornado. We were in the middle of two tornados! I began to pray. I could not contain myself, I just prayed and prayed, and then I began to sing. I sang every possible song I knew. I even sang all the songs they teach you in Cradle Roll. The tornadoes escorted us out of Elizabeth County into the next county, all the while drawing closer and closer to our sides.

Danny's face looked scared for the first time ever. I asked him what was wrong and he responded, "We are on empty. We've been on empty for the past thirty minutes. I have to stop and put gas in." I panicked. "What do you mean, put gas in? Are you crazy? We can't stop." He shook his head and put on his signal lights and pulled into a gas station. I closed my eyes and prayed. The gas attendant came up from the bunker and ran back down. I prayed. The tornadoes just stayed right next to us.

Danny put enough gas in to get us out of there and we continued. It was amazing! Those tornadoes stayed at a safe distance and traveled next to us for over an hour. I thought of that text where God's angels are holding off the winds from the four corners of the earth. As I looked out of my window and prayed, I could sense God's hands holding those tornadoes back. It was our "Red Sea" experience. We praised God when we arrived at Bass Memorial Academy. We shared with the students what had happened, and they mentioned that they had seen and heard about those torna-does. They couldn't believe we had ridden next to them for over an hour. God was truly AWESOME!

A challenge ...

I could write a book on the God-moments we experienced on this trip. I left Southern California with a mission: *Save the Human Race. Share Christ.* I returned a year later recognizing that the only one who truly had been saved was me. God had given me my own story! No longer did I have to sit and just listen to others describe God. Now I could join in and share my very own conversion story! And I did. My life changed completely. I began to travel all around Southern California and around the country. I didn't have great theological conclusions or well-developed sermons. I simply had my story. I spoke of the God I encountered and how He had pro-foundly transformed my life. He had become real. He became not just the God of Abraham and Sarah, of Isaac and Rebekah, but He was the God of Yami and Danny.

Do you long for your own story? Did you know that God longs to give you your very own story? He never intended you to just sit around and listen to other people share about how God is real to them. You remember the story of Joshua and the Israelites, right? Remember when they were about to cross Jordan to take over the city of Jericho? Ellen G. White says that God knew that this young Israelite nation would need not just the story of their grandparents and parents on how God had parted the Red Sea. They needed to see the parting for themselves. And so God did it again. He opened the Jordan and allowed this young nation to experience and see God's intervention with their own eyes. So today, God longs to give you your very own "parting of the Red Sea" experience. But you have to trust Him with your life, your choices, and your future.

A word of caution: when you begin this journey of faith, it will be difficult. Your journey will surely not look like mine. God asks of each of us that which He knows we need to release. For some of you reading this, it might be as simple as terminating a bad relationship. One that you know is killing your soul, but you are hanging on to for dear life and are too afraid to let go. I don't know what God is asking of you, but I do know that He is asking. Since my road trip, God has not stopped. There have been times when I don't want to listen, I don't want to make the necessary changes, I simply am afraid. It is in those times that I pause and reflect on what God did on our road trip and realize that He wants to do even larger miracles in my life, if only I listen, obey, follow, and trust.

A blessing ...

Thank you for letting me share my story. I'd like to leave you, my friend, with a blessing. I pray our roads may cross someday, and I will get to hear how God transformed your life. Until then, may God's ever-present love embrace you and may His grace surprise you today, it is my prayer.

The author is vice president for Student Life at La Sierra University, in Riverside, California.

MILTON CORONADO

"Let's go tagging tonight, bro," I told my younger brother. It was a warm spring night in 1999 when he and I went to bed with the determination that we were going to tag the garage directly behind our house. After a few hours in bed, when the house was silent, I woke him up. I couldn't sleep. The thrill of going out to paint this wall was not allowing me to even stay in one position in bed.

We got up and dressed in our darkest clothes. After grabbing our backpack filled with Krylon and Rusto spray paint, we quietly exited through the rear door and cautiously crept to the garage.

Whenever we painted, we had self-assigned tasks. My brother was the guard, the watchman, looking out for anyone, especially police, while I took care of the actual crime of painting our message on someone else's property, the tag. As my brother stood watch, I quickly painted our crew's name. I painted, "LSP" (Latin Sketch Pride) in seven feet tall script. A crew is a group of people who work on and operate something together. In this case, we would tag together. As I switched cans and filled in the letters, my heart was racing and felt like it was coming up my throat, as if I were falling off a roller coaster. This feeling was half the thrill, an important part of the reason why we did this.

After finishing the tag, I added my brother's name and mine on the bottom corner of the wall. With smiles across our faces, hearts racing, and that hot inner feeling of excitement, we crept back into our house, and into bed.

With pride and convinced of having done something cool, we momentarily left our beds and raced to the window to joyfully accept and contemplate a job well done.

The following night, I remember sitting at our kitchen table, hearing sirens and seeing red and blue lights reflecting in and out of the kitchen. I looked out the window and saw a few police officers taking pictures of my work and writing notes of the crime committed by some "hoodlums" from the neighborhood. The feeling of guilt, shame, and embarrassment was filling me up inside.

Minutes later, they came to our door, talked to my father and my brother, and asked them about the situation. That night my brother took the blame and covered for me. Though I sincerely thanked him and appreciated his action, I didn't stop tagging. I felt if I had done this much and didn't get caught, I could get away with just about everything.

I was rapidly sliding into a life of crime and vandalism. This "drug" of my graffiti obsession was taking control of me and its supplier was Satan. God finally rescued me from a life of self-destruction, but the painful way I learned my lesson is something I don't wish for anybody else.

My mother immigrated into the U.S. at the age of nineteen from Mexico, and took residence in the Windy City, Chicago. While working in a factory she met a man, later married him and had three children. During these years, she suffered emotional and physical abuse. He would push her, punch her, and even broke a few windows with her head.

After a few years of marriage, this man abandoned the family and traveled to California. My mother, feeling unwanted and alone, sought a higher source of hope. She needed God.

Time went by and she met a man at a dance club who had also emigrated from Mexico. This acquaintance developed into something more serious and they decided to move in together. It wasn't too long before she saw the true side of him. She had become free from terrible physical abuse from her previous husband, but now stepped into a higher level of mental and emotional abuse.

You see, if you don't have Jesus in your heart, you cannot truly love. If you don't have love in your heart, it can be difficult to show love towards anyone else. And to show love to her, he needed to take time to know her, her likes and dislikes. Living together without the preambles created more problems than it solved.

These new problems renewed her spiritual journey. In 1979, along with my aunt—her sister—and my uncle, she began to receive Bible studies. Her male companion was stubborn in his Catholic faith and didn't accept them. One year later, I was born into this home. I was followed by a sister ten months later, and another sister three years after her. In that same year, by the power of prayer, my father accepted Jesus Christ. My parents were married and then baptized by immersion into the Christian faith. Here we were, a family of eight going to church week after week, worshiping our Lord with renewed hope, but then Satan had other plans.

On October 5, 1985, my mother fainted in church and was rushed to the hospital. Three weeks later, on October 29, she died from a brain aneurism. Basically, a blood vessel in her head burst. She left behind six children ranging from fifteen years of age to an infant of just twenty months, and now a single, twenty-seven-year-old man to raise them all.

When I became a little older, I questioned God why He allowed her to die. I questioned how things would be if she were still alive. Today, years later, I don't worry about that. I have left that worry along with many others in God's hands. I worry about me and the people I am responsible for. I can relax with the assurance that I will see her again someday. If you have lost a loved one, let God deal with the enormity of your loss. You can't do it on your own. Pray that He'll give you that peace and strength that you need to overcome the troubles that the enemy throws at you so that you can look forward to seeing your loved ones again.

After this tragedy, my mother's first three children moved to my aunt's house, and my father had been left alone with three young children. During the time my father had been receiving Bible studies, he had traveled to Mexico where he met a young girl and got her pregnant. The sad thing about this situation was that my mother found out about his infidelity, and still found the courage to call her husband's lover and offer some help.

My father, to provide a mother for his children and a father to a child left behind, traveled south and came back home with her as a wife, and a new mother and brother for us. This new development created even greater confusion in my mind. I grew up not knowing if this child was truly my brother, and if my father was also his father. This difficult situation triggered a bad relationship between my stepmother and me, which carried over to my sisters. Even though we were attending church, our true colors were shown at home.

Years later, we welcomed a new baby sister, and in 1990, we had a new brother. Now, with a new extended family and some of us entering the teen years, we started to have even bigger problems.

When I entered high school, I got involved with gangs. I also tried marijuana. My teenage life thrived on alcohol, ditching classes, and partying. These were my friends, and the streets were my home.

At that age, most of us feel the need to belong, a group to fit into. We look for love, attention, and acceptance. Those are the kinds of things you're supposed to receive at home from your family, and when you don't receive them there, you will feel a void that needs to be filled with something. Sadly, this is the case with many families today. My father worked very hard, so I couldn't get as much love and attention as I wanted from him. At home it was nothing but yelling, insults, and beatings, so the streets were my comfort.

With hard lessons learned and prayers from those who loved me, I left my gang "friends" but was introduced to the life of graffiti. Ever since I could remember, I've enjoyed art. I used art as a form of escape from my troubled life after my mother's death, so when my peers invited me to employ art to please the group, it was fairly easy for me to agree.

My senior year in high school was a time of experimentation. I drew names and words on sketchbooks and then airbrushed those drawings on T-shirts. Months went by, and by the grace of God, I graduated from high school in 1998. I was accepted to the American Academy of Art, and upon arrival to the school in the fall of that same year, graffiti took over my life. The environment of art and its expression was just overwhelming.

But while I tried to focus in school over the distractions at home and my activities as a graffiti "artist," my father and stepmother were having serious problems of their own. In 1991, they divorced, leaving my father single once again and with six children.

Out of respect for him, I stopped tagging. But after I realized he was coming around and accepting this situation, I jumped back into vandalizing. It was during this time that I painted the garage behind my house along with freight trains in the yards, billboards, and many other public properties, at wee hours like one, two, three o'clock in the morning. I remember being chased by police, dogs, homeless people, and even bullets.

I never forgot about God, and even when I was committing crimes, I really never forgot His laws, or the laws of the land. I knew God still loved me and that He wasn't very happy with what I was doing, but at the same time, I felt He was still with me. In my attempt to try to cover my graffiti addiction, I started getting involved in church.

I thought that if I was involved in church somehow, that made it OK. However, having one foot in the church, as the saying goes, and the other out of it, meant I was not in the church at all. I was physically in the church week after week, but mentally and spiritually, I was out on the streets.

Months went by and to our surprise, my siblings and I found out that my father was interested in a very special Christian woman from Honduras who had plans to temporarily come to the U.S. to work and then go to Mexico to finish her medical education. Well, to this day, she has not gone back! After we met her and noticed the joy she inspired in our father, we accepted her with all our hearts, and soon after, they were married on April 2, 2000. This happy event was followed by the news of her pregnancy a year after.

"Life is good," I told myself. We were attending church as a family. We were praying together. My sister was married and starting her family. College was getting easier and graduation was just one year away. Nothing could go wrong now, right?

The devil thrives in moments such as these. He wants you to think nothing can go wrong, to suddenly surprise you and leave you completely discouraged. He uses your good fortune to tempt you into doing harmful things. He will make sure your life is pretty good, even when you know you're doing wrong. He likes it when you get comfortable at living a double life, only to discover that it really never works. It always ends badly, with losses for both lives.

With all these struggles raging in my mind, I went right back into my comfort zone: graffiti. Only that this time, instead of tagging my name or my crew's name, I was tagging messages like, "God is love," "Jesus saves," "John 3:16," et cetera. The problem is that, although I was writing positive Christian messages, I was still committing crimes and destroying public property. But far more, I was destroying myself. It is pretty scary when you get into the state of mind of feeling unstoppable. That's exactly where Satan had me, but it was also the place where I needed to be to finally be able to see God.

For twenty-plus years my father had been working two or three jobs to support his family. At this point in our lives, through a lot of hard work and God's blessings, my father had built a successful construction company that brought us a pretty comfortable lifestyle. And what's more important, over the years, he had developed a strong relationship with the Lord.

On Sunday morning, September 30, 2001, roughly two weeks after the tragedy of September 11, my dad woke up around 5:00 A.M. to go pick up his employees and go off to work. Just the night before, my father had warned me not to come home too late, since I was going to have to get up early to go work with him, like we did every Sunday. However, on that Sunday of September 30th, my father got up, and contrary to what he had said, got ready, and went to work. It was during this regular job routine that we were again impacted in a way that changed our lives forever.

At six o'clock that morning, two of my father's employees came to my house, picked me up, and drove me to the scene of the accident. As I was getting ready, they mumbled something about my father having been involved in a car accident. The fog was very heavy; in fact, this was the foggiest morning I had ever seen. Objects ten yards away were just a blur and farther out, everything was a smear or simply invisible.

When we arrived at the site, I saw a police officer talking to somebody from the neighborhood. As I came closer, I saw even more police officers and detectives, coming and going in all directions, talking and interviewing more people, and quickly jotting down some notes in their small yellow pads.

Suddenly, I saw my father's double-cabin pickup at the right corner of my field of vision, right next to a tall vehicle. It was surrounded by yellow tape. You cannot imagine the sharp pain that hit me right then. It was as if the pain was running up and down my spine, as if someone was pressing down directly on my nerves, time and time again.

After regaining a modicum of composure, I began to run towards the scene, only to feel a pair of strong arms keeping me from breaking through the yellow tape. It was the unfamiliar arms of a tall gentleman in a long grey trench coat. That's when the interrogation began, question after question; only later did he communicate the unthinkable: "I'm sorry, but your father has been declared dead." He said many more things that still seem all tangled up in my mind, but the one explanation I do remember is, "A bullet struck his head and he died instantly. He really didn't feel anything."

It felt like a lifetime went by, but it was actually a few seconds later that reality set in and I started to kick and punch the vehicles that were parked along the road. A few seconds later, a question began to overwhelm my thoughts: How was I going to tell my family what had just happened? How would I tell my stepmother who was now seven months pregnant?

Just then and there, the Holy Spirit must have taken over, and I say this because there is no way a person can go through this much trauma alone. I can only thank God for helping me to deal with this tough situation.

My father was buried on a Thursday, October 4, 2001. That night, I cried tears I didn't know I had. I lay in bed for a long time; and it was there, in the midst of my pain and utter despair, on a damp pillow filled with mucus and tears, that it hit me: *It should've been me!*

You have to understand something: had I been riding with my father like I was supposed to be, I would have been sitting directly behind him, as I always did. I would have been pretty sleepy and tired from partying the night before, and I would have laid my head on the same window through which the bullet came in and penetrated my father's head.

Something happened that night. Knowing that somehow, for some reason, I had been spared, took over my senses and my thoughts, and on that Thursday night, October 4, 2001, I gave my life to Jesus Christ, 100 percent, once and for all.

I felt a desire, an urge much bigger than me, to see my parents again. And I knew that if that was going to happen, I was going to have to share Jesus with others. I grew hungry for God. All of a sudden, nothing else mattered; all I wanted to do was to share Jesus twenty-four-seven.

This change of heart came right around my graduation from art school, and even though I had bills to pay and dreams of becoming a rich and famous artist, I gave all that up. I made the decision to serve God on a full-time basis. I wanted to be a youth minister.

I wanted to help and inspire young people, especially my brothers and sisters. I wanted to make a difference for people like you. I wanted to help those who have been there with me, overwhelmed by pain and sorrow. The life I had seen so far was so sad and full of pain that I wanted to keep others from seeing what I saw, doing what I did, and experiencing what I had experienced.

By the grace of God, years have gone by and many changes have taken place. I never thought I was ever going to be able to say this, but believe it or not, my life is even better now than it was when my father was alive. It's not that I don't miss him, but there is a lot more peace in my heart, since I have forgiven people that hurt me in the past, including my stepmother.

I stopped tagging and painting graffiti. But just when I thought my tagging days where over, the same God who had been leading my life from the very beginning, the same God who knew how much I enjoyed graffiti, brought me another surprise that has now become a dream come true.

As a function of His incomprehensible love and compassion, God has invited me to keep on painting, but this time to glorify His name. In a marvelous twist of events, God asked me not to stop, but to become even better at it, since I was to do it for Him. After all, the ability to paint and make beautiful art is God-given, and I was to use this ability to share Him with others through art. He could have taken it away, but He evidently had a plan for me.

In 2005, and with the help of great friends, we began a street art ministry. I now minister to young people about Jesus through visuals and street art interpretation. God also blessed me and actually completed me with my wife, Celia. She's a talented, long-time childhood friend and a wonderful companion. God has blessed us with an awesome son, Jaiden Mylton. God has allowed us to have a very cool life; He provides for all our material needs and blesses us beyond belief.

I am currently a youth minister at the Hinsdale Fil-Am Seventh-day Adventist Church, and I know He's not done with me yet, just as He's not done with you either. God will continue to work in us until the final day comes. I know I want to meet Him and finally be reunited with my parents once again.

I now know that God used the challenges I faced and the pain I experienced to build my character. Through these, God has been teaching me to live my life for Him, here on earth and in the future in heaven. I thank God for the parents I had, for teaching me what they did. I thank God for my nine siblings, my brothers and sisters, for supporting and caring for me. I thank God for family and friends, for those who made an impact on my life and always prayed for me. I love them all.

Let me now extend an invitation to you, the reader of these words; better than that, let me challenge you. As a matter of fact, I *double-dog* dare you to meet my best Friend Jesus, to fully accept Him as Lord of your life. I challenge you to honor and respect your parents to the best of your abilities. In spite of the pain and the sadness, in spite of the circumstances of your life, whatever they may be.

After my father died, I felt powerless and unprotected. I didn't know anyone I could depend or rely on, so out of respect for my earthly father, I went to the other Man he always talked about—Jesus. In doing so, I learned who He was and how much He really cared. I learned it was easier than I thought, for it was all about relating to Him as a friend. I learned that it doesn't really matter what others do or say about your faith, or even their faith. What matters is your personal relationship with Him.

I realized that my Eternal Father was telling me time after time to trust Him and perceive Him as the dad I was missing so badly. He wanted me to see Him as the heavenly Father who would be with me always, even to the end of the world. He was with me for the long run, and He wants to relate to you in exactly the same way. You can trust Him; He will not let you down.

If you're reading this, you still have the opportunity to discover the awesome plan God has in store for you. But please understand that the door of opportunity will soon be closed. Today is the time; today is the day to accept Jesus into your heart. You can swear you came across this book by chance, or maybe you think you picked up this book out of curiosity, or because someone pressured you, but no, my friend! You were set up! It was all planned by God way before you were born. It was all a part of God's divine plan to save you, to give you the right to be in heaven; the joy of living in the company of angels, and doing incredible things such as petting a lion[1] and traveling to planets all over the universe.

You'll see and do things you have never imagined.[2] How would you like to see a movie where you are the main actor and your angel is the supporting actor? To see the many times your angel protected you; a movie to glorify the name of Jesus as the story line shows why you belong to heaven through faith and God's grace?

Dear friend, God built a home for you and another one for me[3] with His own hands; I cannot wait to furnish my house, wouldn't you like to furnish yours?

Once you accept Him, give Him all you have. I leave you with one last message. Your abilities are God's gifts to you. What you do with them is your gift to Him. Won't you give Him all?

1. Isaiah 11:6.
2. 1 Corinthians 2:9.
3. John 14:1–3.

The author is a youth minister at the Hinsdale Fil-Am Seventh-day Adventist Church, in Illinois.

IS THERE REALLY A HEAVEN?

JOSÉ CORTÉS

I was saddened when a Christian Seventh-day Adventist teenager said to me, "Pastor, you know what? I don't really care too much about heaven and about Christ's second coming. If He comes and takes everybody with Him and does not take me, that's fine. After all, heaven is a boring place, who wants to go there anyway?"

I became especially concerned because the second coming of Christ is one of the most hopeful promises in the Bible. This world will not be destroyed by a nuclear attack, computer failure, or global warming; Jesus will come and take those who love Him to heaven with Him. This is the reason why those of us who believe in the second coming of Christ, as taught in the Bible, are called Adventists; yet this meant nothing to my teen friend. I can still hear his voice, *"Who wants to go to heaven anyway?"*

I left that conversation saddened, shocked, and determined to go back to my Bible and remind myself about the reasons why I love the second coming of Christ and why I want to go to heaven. Since then, the promise of the second coming of Christ has consumed my life, my preaching, and everything that I do. It all revolves around the fact that Jesus will come again to this earth. He will come as a King to take those He loves to heaven and finally give to them the new earth.

Why is it called the Second Coming? How can I be so sure that

He will come? As an Adventist, I believe in Jesus' first coming. The Bible says that He came once, was born in a manger, lived on this earth, was crucified for us, rose again, and went to heaven. Before He ascended to heaven, He promised He would be back. The fact that He already came once gives me the assurance that He will come again for a second time. But the question remains: So what if He comes? What's in it for me? Who wants to go to heaven anyway?

The first reason why I love the second coming of Christ comes straight from the Bible: "Dear friends, now we are children of God, and what we will be has not yet been made known. But we know that when he appears, we shall be like him, for we shall see him as he is."[1]

I love the second coming of Christ because on that day when He comes, I will be able to see Jesus face to face. Artists have tried to paint Him. They paint Him white, black, Latino, Chinese, serious, smiling, older, younger. Actors have tried to impersonate Him; preachers have tried to explain Him and describe Him so much that at times it can be confusing. On that day when He comes, I will see Him face to face, and WOW, that's awesome!

On the afternoon of December 22, 1997, I found myself at my parents' home in Vineland, New Jersey. I was there on a mission. On that day, I would get to see face to face a young lady, her name was Joanne, from Brisbane, Australia. Joanne seemed to be a wonderful girl; we had written each other lots of e-mails, we both had spent thousands of dollars talking on the telephone, I had some pictures of her, and she had one of my pictures. After communicating for several months, we decided that we wanted to see each other face to face.

I had just started the ministry as a young pastor and in those days, all I had was one week of vacation, and it takes about a week to get to Australia, so it was going to have to be plan B. Her mom and my dad had become good friends, stemming from the fact that my father had been invited to preach several times in Australia. So her mom decided that she would only allow her daughter to travel to the United States if she was to stay at my parents' home.

That's why I found myself at my parents' home on that particular day. Joanne would arrive at the Philadelphia International Airport at around 6:00 P.M. I could not wait to see the girl that I knew, the girl whose messages I had read, and whose pictures I had seen; yet the girl whom I had never seen face to face.

I fixed myself well; I had dark green corduroy pants, and a dark red long sleeve shirt; hey guys, that was in at the time! We got to the airport and waited. The flight arrived on time, the attendants opened the gate, and passengers began to walk out; a big tall dude got in front of me, I kept on looking around him, I could not wait to see Joanne, the girl I knew from pictures and words only. All of a sudden, the flow of passengers stopped. I said to myself, "Oh, she did not make it." Just as I was beginning to worry, a second flow of passengers continued to come out through the ramp's gate, it was a huge Boeing 747. I had forgotten Murphy's law related to picking someone up at the airport: for some reason, our loved one is always the last person to come out.

Most people had already left with their loved ones; passengers were hardly trickling out of the gate anymore. I stood in front of the gate and looked down the exit ramp; I could see the flight attendants picking up their belongings. Once again I worried, "She said she would be on this flight, could it be that she missed it, was there a delay?" Just as doubts were resurfacing, I saw a beautiful shape exiting the plane and walking down the ramp; blue eyes, blond hair, she looked like the girl in the pictures; and there was the million dollar smile, it was Joanne.

I ran to her, she ran to me, we finally met face to face, and I cannot tell you everything that happened at that moment. My father had a video camera, for some reason he only recorded the airport's carpet; my mother had another camera, her pictures only showed the back of my head and they were very blurry. One thing I can tell you, seeing Joanne face to face for the first time was one of my greatest moments.

Can you imagine the day when we meet Jesus face to face for the first time? I picture it like this: I'm walking on heaven's Main Street, a street of beautiful gold, with my sunglasses because of the brightness, holding hands with my wife, Joanne, and my two kids José Cortés III and Joel Benjamin; my parents José and Celia and my brother Josué, his wife, Joyce, and his two daughters Nadia and Emma, we are all there. We are all excited, "That's the angel Gabriel, and that's Father Abraham, and there is Joseph, wow, and Paul, Peter, Esther!"

All of a sudden, I feel Someone covering my eyes with His hands, and I wonder, *Who is this?* I ask, "Is it my friend Roger?"

"No."

"Is it my cousin Ricky?"

"No."

I keep on asking to see who is playing this joke on me, "Who is this?" Then I resort to slowly pulling away the hands that have been covering my eyes for a few moments, and then I see; I see scars in both hands, I know who it is. "Jesus," and He replies, "Yes, José, it's Me, I could not wait to see you here. Welcome to My house." I hug Him and kiss Him and say, "Thanks for watching my back all of these years."

By then my kids are all over Him. "So You are the Big Guy we talked about every morning at worship. You are the One who invented the animals. Can I have a lion?" says José III. "I would like a sea lion," says Joel. "Hey Jesus, where are the baseball fields?" "Can Moses play ball?" "Do You really like the Yankees?" "Did You really save any Red Sox Fans?" It will be some encounter, and we'll make sure we take good video and pictures this time around.

Here is the second reason I love the second coming of Christ: Justin is a twelve-year-old kid who approached me during camp and said, "Pastor José, I am very sad, each time I think of my mom, I get out of control." He went on to tell me that his mom had died when he was five. "I still remember her face, a little bit. I have one picture of her, it's a little blurry, but I don't take it out all the time, because I'm afraid I will lose it." What do you say to a young man going through this?

About a year ago, I stood by the gravesite of a hero. Everyone was crying. The corpse was that of a young man who had committed his brief life to serve our country as a medic and was killed by a roadside bomb in Iraq. His dad, mom, sister, and wife were right there; some of his army companions were there, crying. In this life, no one is truly free from pain. Both the weak and the strong cry on this earth.

Loraine is a young single mom who threatens to take her own life almost every week. Although she has never tried it, she keeps those of us around her constantly scared for her life. Depression can lead anyone to this state. Once, when my wife and I visited her, she told us, "I woke up one night when I was five and my dad was raping me while my mom held me." She continued to tell me, "Pastor José, I feel dirty, miserable, and worthless; it seems that I'm only good to be abused by others, to be taken advantage of. This is why at times I feel I can't take it anymore."

After explaining to her how important she was for all of us, and recommending a great Christian professional counselor, I went to my Bible and read John 14:1–3: " 'Do not let your hearts be troubled. Trust in God; trust also in me. In my Father's house are many rooms; if it were not so, I would have told you. I am going there to prepare a place for you. And if I go and prepare a place for you, I will come back and take you to be with me that you also may be where I am.' "

In the midst of so much hurt, abuse, accidents, homelessness, wars, and deaths, I am reminded that it won't always be this way. We have a place to go to, where there won't be any of these things that hurt us and make us sad. The second reason why I love the second coming of Christ is because it gives me hope. According to Revelation 21:4, " '[God] will wipe every *tear* from their eyes. There will be no more *death* or *mourning* or *crying* or *pain,* for the old order of things has passed away' " (emphasis supplied). I love His second coming because it gives me something that nothing else can give me; I have hope, and you know what? You do too.

I am so glad every time I hear stories of young people who were born in a Christian family and left God and the church in their youth, and after doing all kinds of things and almost destroying their lives without God, they finally see the light and come back to God, their families, and their church. I find these stories dramatic and interesting; each time they keep me on the edge of my seat. But I don't love these stories because of the drama and the suffering endured by these young people while away from God; I love these stories because they show the power, great love, and mercy of God, who is able to forgive and bring back anyone regardless of his or her behavior.

In my case, I never left God and the church. I grew up in an Adventist family and I've stayed here since I was born. At times I feel that I don't have a story to tell. I never did drugs, never been in a gang, never had sex before I was married, never drank alcohol, I wasn't even tempted to play ball on Sabbath in high school!

Although I've had a great time in my life and lots of fun, I feel that my story is not as interesting as others. When these thoughts come to my mind, I am reminded that none of the good things I've done or the bad things I did not do have the power to save me and give me the right to benefiting from the Second Coming. It takes the same amount of power, love, and mercy from God to save someone who has never been in church or left the church, as it takes to save someone who has always been in church.

If you are away from God and your church, stop and please come back. If you have never been close to God, or in His church,

Jesus is calling you today, come. If you never left the church, congratulations; if everyone had left there would be no church. You've helped to keep God's mission going. Don't go anywhere, stay, God needs you right where you are.

If you are part of the group who grew up in the Adventist Church, you know that growing up Adventist is very interesting. I remember several instances in the kids' classes where I was asked by my teacher, "What would you like to do when you get to heaven?" I replied, "I would love to play baseball." You have to understand that all little kids born in Cuba, with very few exceptions, love to play baseball. So baseball was my answer.

My teacher went on to tell me that in heaven we won't have baseball because we'll spend eternity studying the mysteries of eternity and playing the harp. *Oh no,* I said to myself, *study all day and play the harp?* I know my teacher meant well, but you don't tell a five-year-old kid that he will have to give up baseball and study all day in heaven; on a different note, I would not mind learning to play the guitar. "Well, if we don't have baseball, I would like to go swimming in the ocean." My teacher was quick to inform me that in heaven there will be no ocean, to which I replied, "Well, the Bible mentions a sea of glass, with water as clear as crystal. I'll swim there." There is always a funny kid in each class, and this time my funny friend said, "You cannot swim in that sea because it is a sea of glass and you will cut yourself." Once again I thought, *Then ... what do I do in heaven? It's got to be better than just studying all day!*

"Alright, I would like to drive in heaven." As a kid, my dad used to sit me on his lap and let me drive our family car when we drove in a deserted area, that was something I really looked forward to. Once again, my teacher "straightened" things out for me and all of my friends in class. "In heaven," she intoned with a strong voice, "we won't have cars or drive, and we will all have wings and fly." That's not a good thing to say to a male child growing up in Cuba and other Latin American countries; having wings and flying are sometimes synonyms with fairies and those tend to be of the female persuasion. "But I don't want to fly in heaven … how about if I just walk or run fast and never get tired?"

Many of the kids in my generation, previous generations, and present generations have grown up thinking of heaven as the most boring place there is. As I became a teen, I heard someone say that there would be no families in heaven; that we would all be angels. That really bugged me. Now, I know that when it says that we will be like angels it does not mean we will *be* angels; it is talking about the fact that we will lead eternal lives such as theirs. After all, if God wanted us to be angels, He could have made us angels from the beginning. There were angels before we existed. At that time, I could not have imagined my life without my dad, mom, and brother, anywhere. Would the very same God that created the family take it away in heaven? That does not make sense.

Then as I got older, I really began to like girls. Girls seemed so beautiful. In my mind, I remember thinking, *One day I will marry one of these girls and we'll have a beautiful family, and kids, and all, just like my parents.* Then came a hard blow. Someone told me, "People won't get married and there will not be sex in heaven." After studying these subjects deeply, I understand that this comes from one passage found through the Gospels, which it says that at the resurrection people will be rising from the dead, not getting married. I came to understand that this passage is not talking about heaven or the new earth; it is talking about the resurrection. This passage has been taken out of context and mixed with false traditions that have no biblical support, such as the teaching that sex was the original sin.

I know that there are people who teach that getting married is sinful and that sex even in marriage is also sinful. I now know where all of these traditions came from, now I understand that they are not true, that they are just that, false traditions. But as a teenager, I did not know these things and I was horrified by the possibility that Jesus would come and that I would have to go to heaven and live in a mansion with a whole bunch of guys and never be able to get married, have a family, kids, or sex.

Together with a whole generation of young people, I began to wish and pray, "Jesus, please don't come yet … Wait a bit longer, till I am able to get married, have kids and a family, and then, when I get old and cannot enjoy my life and family anymore, then have Your second coming."

The third reason why I love the second coming of Christ takes care of all of these worries, concerns, and traditions. It takes care of everything you've ever heard from people who have tried to make heaven look like a horrible and boring place, when in fact it will be the best, most enjoyable, and fun place for kids, teens, young adults, and adults. Consider 1 Corinthians 2:9:

However, as it is written:

"No eye has seen,
    no ear has heard,
no mind has conceived
    what God has prepared for those who love him."

I also love the second coming of Christ because of the good things He has prepared for us. As you read this chapter, I would like to challenge you to think of all the good things you have ever experienced, dreamed of, or seen on TV, and wish you had the opportunity of enjoying. Of course, I'm referring to those things which are truly and entirely good. When you are done with your list, multiply everything by one million and you may be getting closer to what God has prepared for you.

Here are some of the things I'm hoping for: I will keep my family. My kids will never get sick. I will never argue with my wife. I will swim butterfly-style in the crystal clear waters without suffocating. I will drive fast in really beautiful cars on the Cosmos Inter-Universe Highway. I will teach Moses baseball in exchange for him telling me what it really felt like when he crossed the Red Sea. I plan to enjoy extreme sports without fear, eat heavenly pizza and drink sugarcane juice, and enjoy chocolates without the threat of diabetes. I have a feeling broccoli will be delicious.

I will spend lots of time with my parents and grandparents, but I would love to hang out with God the Father, Jesus, and the Holy Spirit. And I won't mind learning a few mysteries from Them.

In my life as a pastor, I've had the privilege of working with young people for the last seventeen years, in some of the most beautiful and populous areas of the United States and the world: the Washington Metropolitan Area and the New York City area. Through these years, I have experienced the joy of taking groups of young people to other places of the world, where we have been privileged to lend a helping hand, places such as Mexico, Jamaica, Philippines, Dominican Republic, Colombia, El Salvador, the South Pacific, and several countries in Africa.

I have seen hundreds of lives changed by these mission trips, year after year. There are very few things that are as effective in changing lives and creating new leaders as going on a mission on behalf of God to help and save people who need Jesus and need us.

That's exactly what we did in Cojutepeque, El Salvador, in 2002. A group of young people and adults from the Washington, D.C., Metropolitan Area, teamed up under our leadership, with the objective of building the Los Naranjos church, in Cojutepeque.

All forty of us worked very hard through the week; at times we worked all the way through the early hours of the night. We finished our church in one week, bought chairs for the sanctuary, and little chairs for the kids' classes. On Sabbath, both my father and I preached at the brand-new church; it was very satisfying.

CHANGED

On Sunday, our last day in El Salvador, we went sightseeing. We bought souvenirs, enjoyed the capital, San Salvador, ate some pupusas, a delicious Salvadorian dish, and since we all love the ocean and it was a very hot day, we decided to take the group for a swim at Costa del Sol (the Sun Coast).

We ordered lunch at a restaurant, and as we waited for lunch, decided to plunge in the waters of the Pacific Ocean for a swim. We had been in the water for a few minutes, at waist depth, when out of nowhere there was a big wave that surprised us. As the wave hit us, I realized that I no longer could touch the bottom and tried to swim a bit closer to shore. I thought just a few strokes would do it. Great was my surprise when I realized that the more I tried to swim to shore, an undercurrent or riptide, was taking me and our entire group in the opposite direction. Everyone was loudly screaming for help.

Drained by panic, we lost our energies in a matter of seconds. I remember my wife, Joanne, screaming, "Everyone, just swim on your backs!" I began to swim on my back and pray, "Lord, we need Your help. Save our entire group." As I prayed and swam, I lost sight of my wife, Joanne, lost sight of the sand, and began to get really punished by the brightness of the sun and the intensity of the big waves. I looked back and could not see anyone, or anything, just waves, sky, and the bright rays of sun hitting my eyes. I kept on praying, "Lord, please save my wife and our group, and me."

Soon I realized I did not have any strength left, the intensity and the reoccurrence of the waves increased in such a way that I could hardly stay on the surface. I kept on fighting the thought of giving up and just letting myself go, and I kept praying. Then I heard Joanne's voice, she was screaming, "Help, I'm drowning ... Help!" I gathered my meager energies and yelled back, "Babe, don't swim, just float, float on your back, and stay afloat!"

I kept praying for what seemed like hours, but my prayers were getting shorter, "Jesus, save Joanne and me." A few moments later, the prayer was cut even shorter, "Jesus, save me." Then, when I tried to look in all directions again, I saw land. Something I did not know about the riptide is that it is circular; the current takes you out and brings you back in. I saw my friend Felipe, a group member, and someone else getting a hold of my wife; I was partly relieved. Soon after, I realized my feet could touch bottom, but I was too tired to walk or stand, and the current was still hard. I don't know who it was, all I know is that there were two people that grabbed me and led me out to the sand, where I just collapsed.

Through the fogginess of my dulled senses, I heard some voices saying, "There is one more in the water." I did not have any energies, but I kept on praying, "Lord, thank You, save everyone." I gathered some energy and sat on the sand, just as they were bringing my friend, Pastor Brian Han, out of the water.

Pastor Brian Han was twenty-six, a teacher at the academy in New Jersey. Lifeguards began to work on him right away; I got up without any energy and began to pray with the entire group. In my heart I knew, I was sure that God was going to bring Pastor Han back. We all prayed and claimed God's power on behalf of Brian for several minutes. We were willing to pray to God for as long as it was necessary, and we expected Pastor Han to recover.

After forty-five minutes, I was told that my friend and colleague would not make it, he had died. I could not believe it. We had not come all the way from Washington and New Jersey to build a church in El Salvador to leave without one of the group leaders. God could not allow that. As we tried to comfort the young people and give them hope, I thought about instances in the Bible when prophets, Jesus, and the apostles performed miracles.

In that difficult moment, I walked over to where my friend laid lifeless and said to him, "Brian, in the name of Jesus, I command you to rise up." Nothing happened. "Brian, in the name of the Almighty God, who has the power to do anything, come alive!" Nothing happened. "Not by my merits, but in the name of Jesus, who is the Way, the Truth, and the Life, get up and walk." He didn't. I was sure that God would answer and that He would give us Brian back at that very moment. I really wanted him to rise up and walk, but for some reason, God did not give us Brian Han back on that day. And here is the fourth reason why I love the second coming of Christ. It is found right in your Bible, one of my favorite verses, 1 Thessalonians 4:16–18: "For the Lord himself will come down from heaven, with a loud command, with the voice of the archangel and with the trump call of God, and the dead in Christ will rise first. After that, we who are still alive and are left will be caught up together with them in the clouds to meet the Lord in the air. And so we will be with the Lord forever. Therefore encourage each other with these words."

God did not return Brian to us on that sad day in El Salvador, but He will bring him back on the day of the Second Coming. This promise of the resurrection is the fourth reason why I love the second coming of Christ. There is a day, a better day, when Jesus will physically reenter this earth and call Brian and all those who wait for Him in their graves, back to life. The next thing Brian will hear is the voice of Jesus. Brian will not be alone, there will be parents, grandparents, sons, daughters, grandkids, relatives, friends, co-workers who died loving Jesus, and He will wake them up at His second coming. This time, they will all be in perfect health. There will be laughter, happiness, and celebration in cemeteries and graveyards all across the world.

There is a tradition we enjoy with my family, a tradition we have developed for birthdays and other holidays, such as Father's and Mother's Days. On such days, we get up early and wake up whoever is being honored with a serenade of songs. In Mexico and other Latin American countries, serenades are happy occasions, when a lover brings music and songs to the window of his loved one, just before the sun comes up. I look to the day of the Second Coming as a great celebration, a day in which Jesus will have gotten up really early to give those who sleep a powerful wake-up call, and if you think about it, it will also be the greatest of serenades, with heavenly music and beautiful singing.

I love and anxiously await the second coming of Christ because I will see Him face to face, because it gives me hope, because of the "goodies," all of those wonderful things He has prepared for me, and because on that day, I will see my loved ones who have died believing in Him. I can't wait for that day, would you like to help me sing in that serenade?

---

1. 1 John 3:2.

The author is the director of Youth Ministries in the Greater New York Conference area, with headquarters in Manhasset, New York.

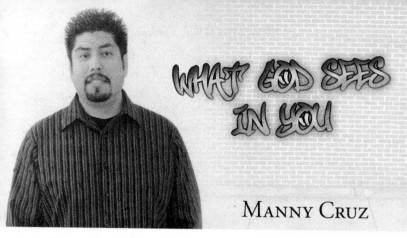

WHAT GOD SEES IN YOU

MANNY CRUZ

Have you ever been rejected? Have you ever felt like you didn't belong? You know what I'm talking about? I do. When I was growing up in the *barrio* in Los Angeles, there were many times when I felt like I didn't belong …

I was born in Tijuana, Mexico, into a family that was not into any church or religion. I remember when my *abuelita* (grandma) María would visit; my father would take all of us to the Pentecostal church because my *abuelita* was Pentecostal. I also remember my mother taking us to the Seventh-day Adventist church a couple of times. Maybe she did this to complement my *abuelita's* Pentecostal influence, I don't know, but a couple times we went to church both Saturday and Sunday.

Other than the few times my *abuelita* would come and stay with us, I don't remember us going to any church on a regular basis. When I was around nine years old, we moved to Los Angeles, California, where I lived until I was eighteen. That first summer in L.A. was hard for me. I did not speak any English and the other kids would make fun of me at the school playground. I felt like I didn't belong. I experienced rejection almost every day.

At home I had four sisters and my mother, and since we lived with my three cousins (all girls) and my aunt, I was the only guy there. My dad worked long hours, so he wasn't home very much. So when I went home from school, I felt like I did not belong there either. Imagine being around nine girls all day! There were times when I just wanted to run away.

I was a Latino kid with not many friends, who just wanted to belong. Around the age of twelve, I started to write graffiti on walls. I don't know why I did it, I just remember doing it. This became my life: writing on walls. For some reason, I became obsessed with graffiti. I knew it was wrong, but I did not care. It was a way for me to belong. I was now a part of the "tagger" crowd in L.A.

Getting involved with "tagging" and graffiti was just the beginning for me. I got caught up with other stuff that I regret today. I realize now how messed up I was, but back then I thought I was "cool." Running around the streets tagging walls felt like the best thing I had going for me. You see, when God is absent from your life, you settle for very little.

Graffiti was my life until the age of seventeen. I am thankful to God because He always had a plan for my life. Romans 5:8 says, "But God demonstrates his own love for us in this: While we were still sinners, Christ died for us." You see, with all the problems at school, the failing grades, the problems at home, and my obsession with tagging, I felt very distressed. I was constantly getting into fights and when I got arrested, I finally realized I was in trouble. It was then, when I felt really miserable, that I turned to God. And the beautiful thing is that God did not reject me! God loved me. God accepted me. God made me feel like I belonged.

It was on January 3, 1987, at the Glendale Spanish Seventh-day Adventist Church that I publicly gave my life to God through baptism. It was one of the happiest moments of my life. I remember Pastor Walter Solís saying to me, *Bienvenido a la familia de Dios* ("Welcome to the family of God"). And I really did feel like I belonged to the family of God.

After my baptism, God just took me on a wild ride. I went to a summer camp that year in Magdalena, Sonora, in Mexico, and the preacher that week was Pastor Armando Miranda. In one of his sermons, he shared the story of a young man who had turned his life over to God and was now a pastor. As I heard that story, I thought of myself and my recent baptism. When Pastor Miranda finished his sermon, he made an invitation for young men and women to come forward. But this was no altar call for baptism or recommitment. He was specifically inviting young people to become pastors. I don't know how or why or when. All I remember is getting up and making my way to the front. I was not emotional or anything, I just thought, *I'm going to be a pastor.*

When I got back home and I told my family and my friends what had happened, most of them tried to encourage me to think about doing something else. They were trying to be nice and not really say, "Dude, you cannot be a pastor! C'mon, be serious, you are not pastor material." I did not care what anyone said; I knew I wanted to be a pastor like the young man in Pastor Miranda's story.

I asked around and a friend told me about the Adventist theological school in Mexico. I called, got all the information, and three weeks later, I was on my way to college. I rode the bus all the way to La Universidad Adventista de Montemorelos, in Nuevo León, Mexico. I spent the next four and a half years trying to pass each one of my theology classes. It was not easy for me since I had never done well in school before. But thanks to God and my friend Josué, who took the best notes in class, I was able to pass most of my classes. Five years later, I graduated with a bachelor's degree in theology.

It took me an extra year to finish because of my grades, but I graduated. Thank God, because—even though I was determined to be a pastor—there were moments when I felt like giving up. After graduation I realized I did not have a call to join the pastoral work. Can you imagine that? Here I was, after working hard to pass my classes, and studying hard, no church wanted to hire me. I felt rejected. Since I was not offered a job in Mexico, I decided to go back to California and look for a job there. Through my father who is a locksmith, I found a job working as a locksmith in the San Diego area. There I was, making keys and replacing locks when in my heart I wanted to preach and work in a church as a pastor.

A few weeks later, I received a phone call from a pastor in Texas asking if I would be interested in working as a youth pastor in a Spanish church. He said I would not receive a full salary, only a small stipend, sort of like part time. The amount was not even close to what I was making as a locksmith, but I didn't care; I wanted to be a pastor so much that I accepted. I had no idea what God was about to do in my life.

I began my pastoral ministry there in a small Spanish church in Mission, Texas. The senior pastor, his wife, his family, and the entire church accepted me and made me feel welcome. I enjoyed working with the young people. But just when I was getting used to things, I received an official call from a conference in Mexico to work full time as a pastor. I was so excited! I went to the interview and some days later, I was riding the bus down to Galeana, Nuevo León, Mexico, to my first "official" church assignment.

I had nine churches assigned to me, and later the conference added five more. I had fourteen congregations and no car. I walked to all my churches and loved it. Whether I walked eight miles or fifteen in the hot sun, in the rain, or at night in the cold, I did not care, I was a pastor! God always took care of me. A few months later, a good friend of mine gave me a truck. What a blessing this was. It wasn't a new truck, it wasn't a stylish truck, it didn't have chromed wheels or spinners, it didn't have a cool sound system, but it got me around to my churches and that's all that I cared about.

During this time, I proposed to my girlfriend Melanie. We had met in college and had dated for four years. She was the most beautiful girl in the world, and now she was my wife. I felt like I was on top of the world. I had my truck, I had a great job in the ministry, and now I had a beautiful wife. I thought life could not get any better, but God had bigger and better plans for my life.

I had been in Mexico working as a pastor for a little over two years, when Melanie and I received a phone call from the U.S. It was a pastor inviting us to come to west Texas and work as an associate pastor in charge of youth ministry in a small church. After prayer and many days of consideration, we accepted.

Soon after our move back to the U.S., I began sharing my testimony with people. I began to challenge teens and youth to get out of their church and into their communities. Many of them accepted the challenge but then asked, What do we do? What can we do? How do we do it? This gave me an idea. Every time I drove through the neighborhoods around town, I noticed the graffiti on the walls. I decided to gather my youth group and start cleaning up graffiti.

I noticed that every time I challenged young people to serve and then offered them the opportunity right there and then, they jumped on it. I think sometimes we as church leaders and pastors don't give our youth the opportunity to serve. We challenge them and encourage them to serve but don't provide them with specific opportunities. So I decided to do this every chance I got.

In July of 2000, I received a phone call from a friend. He said that the North American Division was doing street ministry in Toronto, Canada, and they wanted to include a Street Artists' Ministry, but needed a leader. I told him I had heard about it but was not able to go. He said I should go, and I decided to follow his advice. This is how the Street Artists' Ministry was born. I spent ten days in Toronto teaching a group of Adventist young adults from all over the world how to clean graffiti and paint murals using spray paint. I did not imagine how God would use this ministry to reach hundreds and thousands of teenagers and youth around the world.

After Toronto, I promised God I would share my testimony with as many people as possible every chance I got. So every time I received an invitation to preach at a youth event, I would share my testimony and challenge the youth to serve their church and their community. Several youth groups accepted the challenge, and I would lead them out to the streets of their community to clean up graffiti-covered walls. More and more young people wanted to participate. There were times when we had a large wall to clean up, but so many teenagers would show up that we finished painting in less than thirty minutes. A wall that would normally take one person hours to clean would be done in just a few minutes.

In 2005, in St. Louis, Missouri, during the General Conference session, I teamed up with my friend Josué to lead a group of young adults in the "Impact St. Louis" program. Once again, the North American Division was putting together different street ministries to involve young people in service. Josué and I led a group of youth and young adults from different parts of the world in the Street Artists' Ministry. One of these young adults was Milton. He was an ex-graffiti writer from Chicago who was now on fire for God. As you can imagine, we connected right away. He turned out to be a great artist and a great friend. Together we cleaned up graffiti and painted Christ-centered murals, while sharing our testimonies with people on the streets of St. Louis. Josué, Milton, and I have become partners in the Street Artists' Ministry. Today, all three of us are youth pastors. We receive invitations all over the world to share our ministry. I think we are the only youth pastors in the Adventist Church who still do graffiti. But now we do it for the glory of God! And with permission, of course.

I never imagined what God could do in my life. I never thought that God could forgive me and give me such a wonderful life. In no way did I ever think that God would someday give me a beautiful wife, a wonderful family, and an awesome ministry. It's because I did not know who God was. I had only heard about Him but had never accepted Him.

When I believed and accepted Him, the first thing I learned is that He forgave me. He forgives me, even to this day. That's who God is. That's my God. One of my favorite Bible texts is found in 1 Samuel 16:7 where it says, " 'The Lord does not look at the things man looks at. Man looks at the outward appearance, but the Lord looks at the heart.' " I am thankful for this truth.

When everyone else looked at me and rejected me because they saw a little Mexican kid who did not speak English, God saw a future pastor. When everyone else looked at me and rejected me because they saw a graffiti-writing Latino teenager from L.A., God saw a future leader. When people look at you, they may reject you, but please don't forget that when God looks at you, He sees your heart. He sees the desire you have to be good, to be faithful. Even when you mess up, God sees your heart and how much you love Him, how much you want to serve Him. That is why He forgives you, because He loves you. John 3:16 says, " 'For God so loved the world [you] that he gave his one and only Son, that whoever believes in him shall not perish but have eternal life.' "

The author is an associate director of Youth Ministries for the Seventh-day Adventist denomination in North America. He works from Silver Spring, Maryland.

JOSÉ MARÍN

God has an awesome plan for your life, no matter what cross-roads your are facing today. God has a purpose for your life that is beyond your wildest imagination. It is an abundant life that was dreamed in heaven just for you. Check this powerful promise: "God's ideal for His children is higher than the highest human thought can reach."[1]

And this is true for you too, my friend. God's ideal, His dream, His blueprint for your life is better, and amazingly greater than any human devising. You might be thinking, *Hey, you don't know me, because if you knew what my life was like, you wouldn't be saying any of that; you would then agree that my life has been anything but fair and easy. I have no purpose.* You might think that this thing about God's ideal is just baloney, not meant for everybody, meant only for good kids, those who are lucky enough or maybe have God's blessing on their side.

If you are reading this book, it is because deep down inside you are looking for something different in your life, you are searching for something that will bring you fulfillment. Let me share my story, and maybe, just maybe, you will find a roadmap to God's eternal destiny for you.

When I was born, the circumstances of my birth hinted at a doomed destiny, a future filled with anger, rejection, and low self-esteem. As I grew into childhood and my teen years, I found myself lost, confused, and far from God's ideal. Thankfully, God had another idea for my life, as he does for yours.

I am blessed to have an awesome mother. I come from a family of five brothers and four sisters. My first four older siblings come from Mom's first husband. The other four were born to my mother and my stepdad, who I consider my dad.

It all started one day when my *jefita* (mother) was informed of a terrible tragedy; her first husband had been killed. She had come to the United States of America back in the sixties, looking for a better opportunity and a clearer future. She ended up in the City of Angels. There she met my father-to-be. But there was a little problem. While my mom was pregnant with me and before I was born, my biological father told my *jefita* that he could not continue with the relationship; he was literally giving up on me. He did not want to take responsibility of the child that was about to come into this world. He gave my mother a ten-dollar bill and told her to use it to take care of me.

Even in the sixties, ten dollars didn't buy too many diapers. In other words, my value was set before I was even born; I was only worth ten dollars. I realize that was Satan's ideal for my life, a life worth ten bucks. And Satan has put a price tag on your life and you better believe it isn't much!

What gives me hope is that God has put a price tag on our lives too, check this out:

But now, this is what the LORD says—
he who created you, O Jacob,
he who formed you, O Israel:
"Fear not, for I have redeemed you;
    I have summoned you by name; you are mine. ...
Since you are precious and honored in my sight,
    and because I love you,

I will give men in exchange for you,
and people in exchange for your life."[2]

This is my price tag and your price tag also, you are worth more to Jesus than you can imagine.

Do you know the most expensive gift the Father ever gave His Son Jesus? " 'I have revealed you to those whom you gave me out of the world. They were yours; you gave them to me.' "[3] You belonged to the heavenly Father even before you were born. But God decided to give His Son Jesus the best gift possible in the entire universe and that was YOU, my friend. Don't let circumstances in your life, your past, or other people set your value; your worth was set by God. Only a God that values you so much and loves you so deeply will care enough to have a plan for your life, greater than you can ever imagine.

Let's get back to my story. By now, my mother is in a hospital bed in Los Angeles, by herself, getting ready to deliver a child with an uncertain future. What kind of destiny awaited me? That day in the hospital room, my dear *jefita* uttered a simple a prayer, even though my mom did not attend any church. She prayed a prayer that God has not forgotten to this day: "God, if You help me with this child, I will dedicate him to You, this child will be Yours." That was her prayer.

Prayer can put you on the track to discover your destiny. Praise God for parents who pray. If you have a parent who prays for you, praise God. That mother or father that prays for you is giving you the key to unlock your destiny with God. I was born in Los Angeles, California, on February 9, 1969. So I started life without my father and a mother who was still in the process of healing from the loss of her husband.

Some years went by, and my mother met my stepfather, who soon became my father for all purposes. We moved to San Diego when I was about seven years old. Those early childhood years, and even as a teenager, I found myself wondering why my biological dad had given up on me.

I later learned I was dealing with an identity crisis. I was consumed with trying to understand my true origin and my real purpose in life. I grew up with a sense of rejection, I felt abandoned and lonely. Deep inside, I felt I was perhaps a statistical accident. Have you ever felt confused and tried to figure out why you are here? What is your destiny? I want to assure you that God doesn't treat you as an accident. He has a purpose for each one of us.

Have you ever thought of all the factors that had to be in place in order for you to be born? The same night you were conceived, a miracle took place. Let me attempt to explain it. When you were conceived, an average of five hundred million sperm cells were deposited into your mother's womb! But out of those five hundred million sperm cells, only one made it.

But it gets more interesting. Once that one sperm enters, no other sperm can enter the egg, and later on, all the other sperm cells will die. Do you know what that means? It means 499,999,999 (million) potential combinations were rejected to give way to one potential human being! May I say congratulations? In a sense, you are who you are because a single and "courageous" sperm cell was successful over half a million others! And if you take into account that at least one of every five pregnancies will end up in miscarriage and another one of those four pregnancies will end up in abortion,[4] you should start feeling very lucky that one particular sperm cell and your mother's egg turned out into the wonderful creation that you are.

Going back to my own birth, it's now obvious that my introduction to this world was something much better and bigger than an accident. I had to be planned by God! I was a miracle in God's divine plan! And so are you. You made it this far, your have overcome some hard obstacles, you are here in this world for a reason. The Bible confirms that God has a destiny for your life. "For he chose us in him before the creation of the world to be holy and blameless in his sight."[5]

You were chosen by God before the creation of the world. To be made holy means that God has set you aside with a special purpose.

"For you created my inmost being; / you knit me together in my mother's womb. I praise you because I am fearfully and wonderfully made; / your works are wonderful."[6]

Out of the half-billion possible combinations at conception, maybe even some with greater talents, better looks, or higher IQ, God said Yes to you and me.

Now the question is, Why did God choose you and me? Let's continue with my story to illustrate the answer. Our family didn't attend any church, but God took the initiative to come into our lives. In 1980, an evangelistic meeting came to our town in San Diego. Someone came to our home to share God's Word, then God sent a pastor, Ruben Rodriguez, who visited our home to share God's plan for our lives.

Christ came into my heart when I was only nine. I had the privilege of being baptized with my dear mother. I was so happy, it felt like heaven. There is nothing sweeter and better than the moment when Jesus comes into our lives! Surrendering your life to Christ, letting Him take the lead, is the first step to discover God's plan for your life. Jesus is your future; Jesus is God's plan for your life. You need to come to Christ just as you are. Don't try to change. The whole idea about being transformed is something God does. Your part is to come to Him.

Right when I started to understand that God had a plan for my life, I also discovered such plan was in danger because the devil was opposed to it. My true destiny was almost derailed. School and friends were part of the equation for Satan trying to destroy me. From a young age, I faced significant problems in school, from elementary to high school.

I recall some of my parent-teacher conferences in elementary.

The teacher would begin with, "Your son José is very bright, he's very smart, BUT …" I heard this phrase time and time again. To complicate things, my friends from school started to get involved with drugs, and some ended up in jail. The pressure was coming from different directions.

At church, a large number of my friends were not attending anymore. There were not very many people my age in our church. Church was boring. Saturday nights I would go with my friend who was a disc jockey, and we played music at *quinceañeras* and parties in San Diego and sometimes even in Tijuana, Mexico. Things were not looking good for me at school, with friends, or at church.

In the summer of '84, my closest friends and I became friends with a girl who worked at McDonald's as a supervisor, so every day in the afternoons we went to visit her and get free ice cream. Towards the end of the summer, I was stunned when my mother told me we were moving to a neighboring city for no logical reason. The main reason I was disappointed was that I would have to go to a new school.

Two weeks after we moved, I turned on the television and was stunned as I watched the news; it was from my *barrio* in San Diego. A man had gone into a McDonald's with a machine gun. It was the same McDonald's we would hang out at every day around 4:00 P.M. to get our free ice cream. A madman had shot and killed twenty-one people including some of my friends. I was shocked. The next day I went to the crime scene, which was filled with reporters. I could not believe it.

I realized if we hadn't moved, I would have been there and easily been dead by now. It happened around 4:00 P.M. I was interviewed by reporters because I knew some of the victims. The thought lingered in my mind, *It could have been me.* I was very grateful to be alive.

That following school year, I started ninth grade, but I did really bad in school. I had no motivation, school was hard. I flunked the ninth grade, can you believe that? I decided to give it another try. I did somewhat better and this time I passed.

After the tenth grade, I concluded that school was not for me. I had decided that I was going to drop out at the end of my sophomore year. That summer I got a job at a junkyard. I thought I was going to take out parts from the wrecks, but I ended up carrying huge Cadillac doors on my shoulders, all the way to the back of the yard. It was a hard job, and after the summer was over, I decided that I did not want to do this for the rest of my life.

I finished my junior year, which was a miracle in itself. By the time I was going to begin my senior year, I was invited to attend a Seventh-day Adventist school, San Diego Academy. All my education had been in the public school system so far, but I ended up doing my senior year there. I really had a blast that year. It didn't take long for me to start thinking about my future and to begin to create a dream for my life.

After high school, I wanted to be a border patrol; it was a job that appealed to me. I wasn't trying to be mean to my *raza* (ethnic peers); in a way, I was hoping to be able to help my people. When I told my *jefita* that I wanted to become a border patrol she began to grow concerned, especially because I had to carry a gun. She would tell me, *"No mi hijito, no puede ser posible."* I would reply, "Yes, Mom, it can be possible!"

One day after my *jefita* was very troubled with these thoughts, she heard a voice that spoke to her audibly, *"Your son is not going to be a border patrol, your son is going to be a pastor, and he is going to be an evangelist."* I remember my mom sharing that with me, but I did not pay attention to the supposedly heavenly Voice speaking to her. Me, a pastor? You've got to be kidding!

Spring break was approaching and the chaplain at San Diego Academy invited me to go on a mission trip. There were two obstacles. First, I didn't have the money. I was going to have to get some money to pay for my trip. Second, I needed to get vacation days I didn't have from my work at a child-care facility. I communicated this to the chaplain as the reasons why I couldn't go on the mission trip.

A couple of days before the trip, he asked me if I still wanted to go. He then explained how an anonymous person had paid my way for the mission trip. Can you believe that? Eventually, I was able to get permission from work and off I was to Mexico. Since there were only a couple of Hispanic kids, we were asked to lead certain teams and to translate worships and Sabbath services.

I still remember to this day one very special night, out in the middle of the desert, under a sky lit with stars. I looked up to heaven and began to wonder exactly what kind of plan God had for me, what His purpose was for my life. I started thinking how much fun I was having there. There was real joy and a complete satisfaction and fulfillment in ministering, and in building a church for God.

That night as I looked towards heaven, a conviction crept into my heart and whispered in my mind: *"Son, this is what I want you to do for the rest of your life."* That night I felt God's call to serve Him on a full-time basis. I went back home with the decision of becoming a minister. I went from border patrol to an individual dedicated to "catch" as many people as I could in order to "sneak" them across the "border" into heaven!

That was it! That was my purpose. I came into this world not by accident. I came with a mission to serve and to save. I don't know why God chose me, but He did. My dream was to become a border patrol. Dreams are always good, for they give you a sense of direction, but when you finally discover the dream God has for your life, a new path begins to unfold before you. Something you never thought possible. Go on, dream, discover your dream, but more than anything, discover your ultimate destiny with God, the reason God chose you to come into this world.

Listen to the words of Jesus; here's the purpose He had in His life here on earth: " 'My food,' said Jesus, 'is to do the will of him who sent me and to finish his work.' "[7] This is also your ultimate purpose in life: to know God, to do God's will, and to finish the work for which He has called you. For only this will bring fulfillment to your life. Only this will bring real joy and a deep encounter with Jesus Christ.

When I got home from my mission trip, I told my mom the exciting news of my decision to become a minister. She began to cry and a few moments later, she reminded me of the dream. The dream where God assured her I was going to be a pastor, not a border patrol agent.

I told my friends and my church family, and no one could believe it; neither did I. That is exactly the way God works; He takes the weakest of the weak to manifest His power in spite of our inabilities.

God has called you not because of who you are or the strengths and skills you possess, but rather because of His power and His love to transform you and equip you for the tasks He will have you perform. God elected you first, He chose you to be the first player of His team! He knows you and gives you a destiny higher than any of us could ever imagine.

I joined the Seminary and began my preparation to become a minister at Montemorelos, the Mexican theological school. That became an unforgettable experience in itself.

During my freshman year in college, I met a beautiful and wonderful girl by the name of Cynthia; love happened and we got married on August of 1992. I can honestly tell you that even our marriage was born in the heart of Jesus. God knew our needs and led us to one another. Cynthia loves the Lord and we share a passion for the lost that has brought us together even more. Through her, God has brought a lot of happiness to our home, especially with the arrival or our three incredible kids, Geovanni, Nephtali, and José Miguel.

My life has not been perfect, but it has been an adventure with God that I wouldn't trade for anything, and I know He is not finished with me just yet. I have been working as a pastor and evangelist since 2003. By the way, I never learned who paid for my mission trip, but I know the Voice my mother heard on that blessed evening was truly the voice of God.

Jesus means everything to me. Most children who are abandoned by their biological fathers are prone to failure, but I had the privilege of knowing a Father in heaven who wanted to become active in my life. Although a ten-dollar price tag was set for me, God purchased my salvation with the precious life of His Son Jesus, whom I can call my Big Brother! Jesus has done so much for me; He has given me more than I could ever imagine. He has been so good to me, that I don't have words to articulate my gratitude.

What about your life, my friend? It doesn't matter where you come from, your background, your education, or the lifestyle you are now leading. What matters is that you understand that an amazing God loves you and has a plan for your life that challenges any imagination. No matter how messed up your life is or how good it is, with Christ it can be better.

You might be asking, Where do I begin? What steps do I need to take? The good news is that before you take any step, God has already taken the first and the last step towards you. You are not an accident; if you made it this far, your life is a miracle.

There are two questions that you must answer in your quest for meaning that will help you find your ultimate destiny. Paul the apostle asked these questions to Jesus when he came face to face with his destiny: " 'Who are you, Lord?' "[8] and "Lord, what do You want me to do?"

The first question is an invitation to get to know Jesus in a personal way. The answer to that question will lead you to spend time in His presence. Take some time every day to read your Bible, even if it seems boring at first, for it will change soon into a craving for God's Word.

If you haven't surrendered your life to Christ, make the deci-

YOUR ULTIMATE PURPOSE

sion today to let Christ be the ultimate Master of your life; let Him guide you. Your destiny begins and ends with Christ, " 'I am the way and the truth and the life.' "[9] " 'Now this is eternal life: that they may know you, the only true God, and Jesus Christ, whom you have sent.' "[10] You may not know at this very time what the purpose of your life is, but surely Christ, the One who created you, the One who chose you does know. Spend time every day with Jesus in His Word and in prayer.

The second question is aimed at helping you discover the reason God brought you to this world. Here's what Paul said: "God, who set me apart from birth and called me by his grace, was pleased to reveal his Son in me so that I might preach him among the Gentiles."[11] You were set apart by God from your mother's womb, you were called not because of who you are, but according to God's grace. Your call in life is to preach the goodness of Christ. " 'Before I formed you in the womb I knew you, / before you were born I set you apart; / I appointed you as a prophet to the nations.' "[12] Before you were conceived, God already knew you; He knew everything in your life. You were set apart with a special purpose, and that purpose is to know God and share with others about God's amazing love.

Ask Christ what His will for your life is; ask Him to lead you to the destiny for which you were created. Believe me, God is desperate to answer that prayer! After all, Christ is the One who brought you into this world with a purpose. Pray to God that He will show you the way. Believe He will, just have faith and be patient. Once you find your purpose, decide to serve God for the rest of your life. Tell your friends what God has done for your life. Tell them about your experience with Jesus. Help your friends come to know God's ultimate plan for their lives, as you help them meet the One who is the Way, the Truth, and the Life.

Last year I went to Mexico to have evangelistic meetings in a church in the southern part of the country. A man from church asked me at the end of the service if I could pray with a little seven-year-old

C—4   • 97 •

girl, so after the service we went into a separate room with the man, the little girl, and her grandmother. I looked into the eyes of this child of God, I placed my hand on her little head, and I told her, "God loves you. God has a plan for your life. You are special to God." The little girl started to sob. Then I went ahead and prayed over her, I affirmed God's love for her, and I asked God to lead her to her ultimate destiny.

After the child left, the brother from church told me that the reason why the grandma wanted me to pray for this little girl was that two days earlier, she found the little girl trying to commit suicide. I couldn't believe it. Then he went on to tell me that both mother and father had abandoned this precious child. The little girl had been saying for the past weeks, "No one loves me. My mom and dad don't want me."

Even now, I pray for her to understand there is Someone who loves her. I pray that she will be able to understand that God selected her, that she is not an accident. Even as she deals with the terrible pain of rejection, I pray for her to discover her ultimate destiny in God's loving hands.

My friend, remember that God loves you very much; you are not alone, He will never abandon you.

"Can a mother forget the baby at her breast
    and have no compassion on the child she has borne?
Though she may forget,
    I will not forget you!
See, I have engraved you on the palms of my hands."[13]

He is with you and will guide you to a life with purpose, if you let Him. Live each day with Christ, let Him fulfill His will through you, and soon you will see Jesus face to face, the One who selected you even before you were born.

1. Ellen G. White, *In Heavenly Places* (Washington, D.C.: Review and Herald® Publishing Association, 1967), 141.

2. Isaiah 43:1, 4.

3. John 17:6.

4. Anthony DeStefano, *Ten Prayers God Always Says Yes To* (N.Y.: Doubleday Publishing, 2007), 166, 167.

5. Ephesians 1:4.

6. Psalm 139:13, 14.

7. John 4:34.

8. Acts 9:5, 6.

9. John 14:6.

10. John 17:3.

11. Galatians 1:15, 16.

12. Jeremiah 1:5.

13. Isaiah 49:15, 16.

The author is the leader of Hispanic Ministries in Arizona, and writes from Phoenix.

ELDEN RAMÍREZ

I remember as if it were yesterday, when two gentlemen came to my house to communicate to my mother that my father had passed away. Since I was only five years old, it was very hard for me to understand what had just been told to my mom. It was the first time I had ever seen my mother cry so much. That night she tried to explain to me what had taken place by saying, "*Mi hijo* [My son], your father is not coming home anymore."

At first I was under the impression that my dad was not coming home that particular night; however, later I would learn that he would not be coming home for the rest of my earthly life. I don't remember crying that night, for I did not understand the meaning of death. I don't recall having any sad thoughts other than my father was not there that night to share with me a bedtime story.

During the next few days, things changed. Not having Dad home the subsequent nights was not fun, and later going to my first funeral service was the hardest thing I had ever gone through. It was not until I saw my father lying inside his casket that it finally sank in, and I realized that he was gone and not coming back. I spent the entire funeral service next to his casket. I was crying nonstop and at times I cried hysterically making things a lot more difficult for my mother, who was also taking care of my ten-month-old sister.

When it was time for the burial service, I did not want to let go. I knew that shortly the "ground" would take away my dad and I would not see him again. I held on to the casket for as long as I could, but time was running out and it was time for him to go and be placed underground. I began to cry so much that my mother decided that it was best for me to stay at my grandmother's house and not attend the burial service.

That afternoon I started wondering how life was going to be without my dad. I knew it was not going to be easy; however, little did I know that the worst journey was about to begin. I remember crying myself to sleep that night. Every day after that was a struggle and every night a desperate cry.

Christmas came not too long after that. It was the saddest Christmas ever. My mom did everything in her power to make it special. She bought my sister and me a lot of presents and every single one of them was great. I remember her buying my first collection of Hot Wheels miniature cars and a new pair of cowboy boots. It would have been the best Christmas ever if my dad had been there. I knew how much it hurt my mother to see me cry, so I would hide in my room. Later in life, I found out she did the same. She would never cry in front of my sister or me, but often she would go to her room and cry before the Lord.

As the months went by, you would think that my pain would go away, but it was still there and it was not getting any easier. My birthday soon came around and like Christmas, my mother had prepared the best birthday party yet. All the neighborhood kids and my cousins were there to celebrate my sixth birthday. As I look at the pictures today, I can only imagine how difficult it must have been for my mother to prepare this celebration without my dad. She was only thirty-three years old, and was doing her best to bring a smile to her children.

I praise God she was strong for us and did the best she could, but I still missed my dad greatly. Perhaps what I missed the most about my dad was his smile while playing the marimba. You see, my dad was very silly, and often times he would play the "Happy Birthday" tune on my toy marimba, even though my birthday was on a different date. He would do this just to see me wake up with a smile on my face. To him, every day was a celebration.

The year after my father's death, I attended pre-kindergarten and experienced what would become the worst holiday of the year, Father's Day. Every year, teachers would ask the class to make a "Happy Father's Day" card for our fathers. The first time I was asked to celebrate this holiday, I remember resting my head over my desk and crying desperately. My teacher was very nice and kind to me. She pulled me outside the classroom to inquire what was wrong. After we talked for a while, we went inside the classroom and while the other kids where working on their cards, she helped me come up with a card that read "Happy Father's Day, Mom." That was the first of many that I would make during the following years.

As a child growing up, I became very angry toward death because "it" had taken away my father when I needed him most. Shortly after that, I attended my grandmother's funeral and a few years later, my uncle's. Often I would question God and ask Him why He allowed death to come and take away those whom I love. Eventually, I became desensitized to death; I was not afraid of dying, nor cared if I did. In fact, sometimes I felt the sooner "it" came for me the better.

There is no doubt I was hurting and in great need for inner peace. It was in the middle of this chaos that a wise Christian man came into my life. It was my great-grandfather, an old Adventist missionary who took me under his wing and began to answer the many questions I had. I don't know where he had been all this time. I assume he was always there but I had never noticed him, until he began to come home every afternoon to help me with my schoolwork. It appears to me that he was just waiting for the right time to facilitate a healing process that would change my life forever.

He read the Bible to me daily and would fill my heart with God's promises. I would look forward to spending time with him every afternoon. That year I made two "Happy Father's Day" cards, one for my mother and one for him. The pain was slowly going away and peace began to fill my heart.

Every day my great-grandfather would share with me a Bible truth that would reveal the character of God. I was no longer angry with God, for I had finally understood that He loved me beyond measure and He had plans for my life.

Just when things started to turn around, my great-grandfather suffered a horrible accident and became very ill. My great-grandfather was 103 years old at the time and there was uncertainty as to how long he would live. I knew that he was probably not going to make it, but I had learned from him the importance of prayer and how we could go to God in the midst of our troubles. I asked the Lord to allow me to keep him for just a little while longer. There were still many questions I had to ask him and Bible studies to finish. I remember praying fervently that night and falling to sleep on my knees.

Miraculously, my great-grandfather got well and was able to walk out of the hospital. He continued to spend every afternoon with me studying the Bible for the next three years. He passed away in his sleep when he was 106 years old.

Once again, I was standing before a casket seeing another loved one going to their resting place. However, this time it was different, I was sad but had a great sense of peace. My great-grandfather had taught me to trust in God's promises. I knew that death was not the end of the road, and I was convinced that I would see him again. It was then that I began to long for the second coming of our Lord. I wanted to see again all of those who were resting. I knew that there was more to life than this sad and hurting world.

CHA NGED

My mother eventually got remarried to a retired minister who loved the Lord. He became a friend and a father who also shared with me life-changing lessons that one day would become priceless. It is evident that throughout one's life, God always places people in our path that help us see His will for our lives.

Later, during my tough teenage years, I remember a godly pastor who came to our church. There was something special about him. At first I could not figure it out. His sermons must have been great, for people would love to hear him speak. The church got so full that another church was born. Later, I realized that what made him special was not just his sermons, but the fact that he cared.

As a young teen, his ministry blessed me. I don't remember any of his sermons but I remember clearly every single act of kindness and compassion. It is amazing how everything began to make sense. It is as if the Lord was sending a messenger for each chapter in my life. When I was hurting as a small child, God sent my wise great-grandfather; during my early teens, my stepfather; and as a young adult, a godly pastor, and each one of them complemented my mother's efforts to raise her children.

As much as I would like to say that everything was great after that, I can't. My high school years were very tough. I attended what at the time was considered the worst high school in the district. The first thing I heard was the news of a young man that was hung from the basketball hoop by a rival gang. I never knew if this was true, but the school sure had a horrible reputation.

We had security guards on every floor. There was graffiti all over the bathrooms. Every day the janitors would clean the walls, but almost immediately, there was writing all over them again. Writing schoolwork using graffiti handwriting was acceptable by some teachers. "As long as you turn in your schoolwork, it's OK," one of my teachers would reply, when asked if this was an option.

Teachers did everything they could to motivate their students. The reality was that finishing high school was not an achievable goal for many of my friends. Being able to finish the day alive was their immediate goal. I remember the first time I experienced a drive-by shooting. Everything happened so quick that when it was all over, I was just glad that my friends and I were still alive.

I know things have not changed much in America. Just today I was reading that 50 percent of all drive-by shootings in America happen in California. In July 2006, there were a total of 549 drive-by shootings in the U.S. It's no wonder many students don't want to go to school. In fact, in a *60 Minutes* program they reported that over one hundred thousand kids each day won't go to school, because they're afraid that something may happen to them. There were days that I too skipped school because I was afraid. Some days it would appear that different gangs controlled every section of the school building. It is under this environment that you learn the rules of survival.

Many times, I was afraid that I would make a wrong decision that would lead me down the wrong path. I knew that my mother would suffer beyond measure if something would happen to me. This was the main reason I remained out of trouble and in school. I had seen my mother suffer so much, and I was not going to cause her any more pain. I wanted to make her proud. I dreamt of becoming someone influential that would honor her by my actions. But, what was to become of me? What was I going to do with my life?

I often asked God to show me His purpose for my life, because it was so hard to see His plans. Many of my friends began to drop out of high school; others were arrested. By the time I was a senior in high school, I had caught up to my best friend who was a year or two older than me and started school earlier than I did. As I look back in time, toward the end of my high school year, it was just him and me standing before an uncertain world. Again I found myself asking, "What is to become of me?" "What am I going to do with my life?"

As I travel to several countries speaking at youth rallies, I constantly find young people who are hurting, longing for peace, wondering what the meaning of life is. There is no doubt we all go through challenging times in our youth, and sooner or later, we all ask the same questions: What is to become of me? What's the purpose of life? Someone asked me the other day, "When did you find your life's purpose?" I wish I could have pointed to a specific time and day—maybe a dramatic moment—however, I realized that it was a sequence of events that lead me to the answer for his question.

After my great-grandfather's death, I developed a great desire to serve the Lord, to pick up where he left off. I struggled with the idea of becoming a missionary, but somehow during my years in high school, my priorities changed, my best friend and I decided that after high school we would go to college to study business and develop an empire together; little did I know that God had other plans for me.

In the meantime, I worked as a young civic leader at San Francisco City Hall, serving in the Mayor's Youth Forum, now known as the San Francisco Youth Commission. It was a great learning experience and I began to seriously consider the possibility of following a career in politics. I was part of a citywide leadership program that provided ideas on youth issues and worked with city gangs to stop youth violence. I was honored to work with a great team of youth leaders who developed public policies for children and youth.

I also worked as an activities organizer with RAP (Real Alternatives Program), a multiservice program for at-risk students. There, we worked with the educational and recreational programs that served the Mission District; providing counseling, orientation, and working with high numbers of young drug addicts.

Just when I thought I had it together and had found the purpose of my life, the unexpected happened, and once again I was faced with "death." My best friend's cousin was murdered, and right after his funeral, my friend began to ask what would become of his cousin. He knew that I attended church on a regular basis and knew that I would have some answers. As much as I wanted to remember the Bible verses that would give him hope and peace, I couldn't, I felt helpless.

Somehow all the years attending church were not enough. I knew what the Bible said about the state of the dead but I could not find it anywhere. I began to talk to my pastor and my stepdad and both helped me with the answers I needed. They both coached me in giving my first Bible study. I was able to share with my best friend the wonderful promises of God; the same promises that one day my great-grandfather shared with me and gave me peace when I was suffering the loss of a loved one. It was then that I realized that I was called to do this for the rest of my life.

By God's grace, I finished high school and graduated with my class. On graduation day, I shared with my friends the good news that I would go to college to become a minister. Unfortunately, I did not get the response or support that I was expecting from them, but I was determined to follow God's lead. It was not easy, but I was convinced of God's calling.

I arrived at college not knowing what to expect, but it was there that two great things happened in my life: I met a beautiful nursing student who would eventually become my wife, and God placed in my life another godly man who became an inspiration and turned into another spiritual father who would guide me as I sought God's will. My four years of college went by quickly, and God allowed me to graduate and become a pastor. Since then, I have served in three different states as academy chaplain, youth pastor, senior pastor, church planter, and departmental director in the areas of family life, health and temperance, the National Servicemen organization, and youth ministries.

As I look ahead, I'm not sure in what other capacities God will have me serve Him, but I'm always ready and willing to go wherever He may lead. Throughout my life, there is one thing I have learned and that is: God does not waste your pain. In every trial and tribulation, God is right there with you. He will never leave you nor forsake you. Every time you feel that there is no tomorrow, or whenever you feel you can't keep going, remember, the darkest part of the night is right before dawn. As Christians, we may be helpless but we are never hopeless. God definitely has a purpose for your life.

As I look at the current situation of our youth in North America, I am troubled when I read that every two hours and fifteen minutes a young person commits suicide in the United States. It seams that too many times, when young people find themselves in helpless situations and with no other options, they end up taking their own lives as the only solution to their problems. After sharing a glimpse of my story, I pray that if you find yourself at a crossroads and find no purpose in life, or perhaps you are facing a challenge so difficult that you have been crying yourself to sleep, you will say like King David,

> I lift up my eyes to the hills—
>   where does my help come from?
> My help comes from the LORD,
>   the Maker of heaven and earth.
> He will not let your foot slip—
>   he who watches over you will not slumber;
> indeed, he who watches over Israel
>   will neither slumber nor sleep.
>
> The LORD watches over you—
>   the LORD is your shade at your right hand;
> the sun will not harm you by day,
>   nor the moon by night.

> The LORD will keep you from all harm—
>> he will watch over your life;
> the LORD will watch over your coming and going
>> both now and forevermore.[1]

There is no doubt God will watch over you. If you trust in the Lord, He will turn your sorrows into joy, "instead of ashes, / the oil of gladness / instead of mourning, / a garment of praise."[2]

At the moment you are going through your trials, it's impossible to see what's ahead, but if you patiently wait on the Lord, the outcome will be indescribable. The other day my seven-year-old daughter sat on my knee and asked, "Daddy, what's your favorite holiday?" As I thought for a minute, I was moved beyond words when I realized that my favorite holiday now is Father's Day.

Every year my little ones give me a "Happy Father's Day" card created with their own hands. I have kept all of their drawings in my desk, and when I face difficulties in my life, I simply open that special folder where I keep their priceless artwork to remind me that if I only wait and trust in the Lord, my pain will eventually turn into joy. As I look back in time, who would have thought that my worst holiday of the year would later become the best one?

There is a chance that, as you read this book, you are facing the worst time of your life, and the pain may be so severe that perhaps you have contemplated taking your own life. If that's the case, please give the Lord a chance to work wonders in your life. Allow Him to do what He does best. To restore that which is broken and to pick up the pieces that life has shattered. At the end of the road, you too will have the ability to say, "Praise God for His goodness, His love endures forever."

---

1. Psalm 121.
2. Isaiah 61:3.

The author is director of Youth Ministries for the Central California Conference of Seventh-day Adventists, located in Fresno.

A WALNUT TREE AND A CHURCH IN THE FRONT YARD

SERGIO TORRES

My name is Sergio Amador Torres Barraza. The Barraza is for my mother's side of the family. My mother's name was Celia Azucena Barraza Pérez. Torres comes from my father's family. My father's name was Amador Torres Torres. As you can see, I take two of my father's names. I have two older brothers, Irvent Rolando and Ulises Roberto, and three younger siblings, two sisters and a brother: Cristina Aracely, Cinthya Carolina, and Guido Alberto.

My brother Irvent Rolando carries the names of my mother's youngest and older brothers. Both had a special place in her heart. By the way, Irvent is pronounced "Ur-vant," as in French. Since my maternal grandmother's last name was Duval, my oldest brother thought that made him French. Cinthya's middle name, Carolina, was given to her because my mother had a great admiration for President John F. Kennedy, who was assassinated the year Cinthya was born. So she carries his daughter Caroline's name. Guido, my youngest brother, was given Alberto as a middle name for a cousin that my mother loved dearly.

Like many people who name their children after someone they would like to honor, my mother chose the names of other people for us to somehow connect her life to theirs. It was as if she didn't want to let them go. As if she wanted to be linked to them through us. So every time she would see us, she would remember them. There was a connection.

I was born in Ovalle, a small town in Northern Chile. So, *soy chileno.* Chile is the string bean country that extends about twenty-six hundred miles from Arica, at the border with Peru in the north, and ending in Punta Arenas in the south. Chile shares its borders with Peru, Bolivia, and Argentina. This is my country. OK, enough of genealogy and geography!

Life in *El Sauce*

It must have been a year or two after I was born that we moved from Ovalle to Santiago, Chile's capital. My parents and my mother's family bought a lot in *El Sauce* (The Willow), a suburb in the southern part of Santiago. When we arrived, we lived with our grandparents, while Dad built our house. It did not take a long time to build this house. It was a simple wood-framed house. It had two rooms. There was one bedroom where we all slept: Father, Mother, the three boys, and our baby sister Cristina. Cinthya and Guido would come years later. The other room was the living/dining room. In the back of these two rooms was the kitchen, which was almost completely exposed to the elements.

The two rooms were insulated with a brown-bag colored paper. This insulation kept the freezing wind out of the rooms during Chile's harsh winters. One of the things that kept us warm was a *bracero* (a small rectangular steel box) that my parents would fill with coal and fire up, so we would enjoy its warmth. As soon as we fell asleep, they would take it out of the room, so we would not die of carbon monoxide poisoning. The other thing that kept us warm was the numerous heavy wool *frazadas* (blankets) that were layered on us. Literally, you were bound to one position all night long because there was no way to turn with such a heavy load!

Our bathroom was an outhouse with a septic tank behind the main house. There was no running water, therefore, no showers.

We had to walk to a nearby street corner where there was a city waterspout and carry the water back to the house in five-gallon buckets. Mother would bathe us by warming up the water and, one by one, putting us inside a big drum for a hot bath. The floor of the house was *terra firma,* a plain dirt floor. I remember as a child sweeping the floor. My mother taught me to sprinkle the floor first with water and then sweep. Our dirt floor was always spotless. Many times, when I think about my childhood days, I go back to that house. Though we were poor, we had a home. It was a warm place.

There are two things that distinctly stand out in my mind about those days in that house. One was a walnut tree in the front yard. This tree was very tall and very fruitful. I really enjoyed climbing its strong branches and hiding way up there. I also enjoyed its shade during hot summer days. The other was the church that was started in our yard. Since there was no church in El Sauce, my mother and a group of her young adult friends from La Cisterna church decided to plant one there. She belonged to the "Club 120," which brought together young adults who really wanted to make a difference for God's kingdom, just like the 120 gathered in the upper room during Pentecost in the early Christian church.

I remember how enthusiastic and passionate these young adults were about their faith and about how Jesus could change people's lives. As a child, it was exciting to see my mother so passionate about God, service, and evangelism. Of course, I didn't know any of those terms. I just saw Mom and her work for God.

My mother convinced my dad to allow her to start the church in our front yard, right under the walnut tree. My dad was not a Christian or an Adventist, yet he was always supportive of our Christian upbringing. Why would he not support a church-planting project in his own front yard? This church-planting project was my first real introduction to church life. Here's why: along with my siblings, we became little helpers. We would be the ones to set up the old wooden chairs and the mimeographed songbooks (the way things were done before photocopiers came along).

The speaker was *el Hermano Silva* (Brother Silva), an enthusiastic and dynamic speaker who would arrive every Sunday evening on his three-cylinder microvan equipped with his Bible, filmstrip projector (long before slides and videos), and a white sheet for a screen. We would sit there, along with neighborhood kids and adults, to hear what *el Hermano Silva* had to say. I remember that some of our neighbors gave their hearts to Jesus and became founding members of what would later be known as *La Iglesia Adventista de El Sauce* (The Seventh-day Adventist Church of El Sauce), right in the front yard of our house.

My parents ended up donating the lot and a church was built there. Remember the walnut tree? Well, the tree was cut down and the trunk was the only thing that survived. It became the pulpit. The wood-frame church was built around the trunk. It was beautiful to see that trunk there. It was so familiar and confusing at the same time. It was familiar because it had been our tree … my tree. It was the tree I had spent countless hours playing on and climbing. But, it was also confusing. For a time, I wondered how a tree could go from being something you played on and had fun on to something sacred. The same trunk was now *intocable* (untouchable) by children's hands. And it was the only pulpit the church had for many years.

Going north to *los Estados Unidos*

It was a cold and rainy winter morning in Santiago, Chile, in June of 1963. Our entire family was up very early that morning. We were heading to the airport where Dad would embark on a fourteen-hour flight to New York. Dad had secretly planned this trip without telling anyone, not even Mother. For years, he had worked in the American-owned copper mine companies in northern Chile and then in foundries in Santiago. He loved working with American engineers. It was there that a dream was born to take his family to *los Estados Unidos de Norteamérica* (the United States of America). With the help of those engineers, he secured a visa. And on this cold and rainy morning, he was making his dream come true. I was ten years old. It would be two years before we would be reunited.

On June 15, 1965, we embarked on our own sixteen-hour flight from Santiago, Chile. After making stops in three different countries, we landed in Miami and waited for several hours for our connecting flight to our final destination, New York City. I was twelve years old and didn't speak a word of English. Neither did my siblings. In a strange country, my mother held us by her side, as a hen protects her chicks. A beautiful blond, blue-eyed flight attendant helped us as we went through immigration and then on to our connecting flight. She was the typical kind, sweet, and smiling woman you'd see on black-and-white American movies back in Chile. She welcomed us to the United States of America and left a lasting impression on our lives.

When we arrived at JFK International Airport in New York, Dad was nowhere to be found. Somehow, with the many last-minute changes, Dad had not gotten the final word from Mom that we were arriving that day. And he was not waiting for us. There we were, all alone. It was 3:00 A.M. by the time we got to the fifth-floor apartment where Dad lived in the Bronx. And what a beautiful apartment it was! It was in that apartment, that early morning, that we got our first real introduction to the American life. When we opened the refrigerator, there they were: a box of Oreo cookies and Coca-Cola bottles waiting for to us to enjoy (no cans then!). We devoured and drank everything.

Life in *los Estados Unidos de Norteamérica* was not easy for our family. My dad worked as a plaster man. I don't know how many apartment buildings in the city he plastered. He was an artist. He could turn old and ugly walls or ceilings into a smooth surface ready to be painted. Soon he discovered that he could be his own boss and found a position as a "super" or "superintendent," as they call building managers in NYC. He became *el Super* of the building located at 415 Claremont Pkwy, just across from where we lived, on the other side of Claremont Park.

The supers always lived in the basement apartments with their families. It was totally different from the fifth-floor apartment we had been living in. No wood floor, only linoleum. But it was home for us. As a super's family, we had tasks to do. On Fridays, in the cold NYC winters, my responsibility was to make sure that the boiler room had enough coal to keep it running for the tenants. My parents taught us we did not have to be hauling the coal from another room on the Sabbath. All Dad had to do during the Sabbath was just open the boiler and shovel the coal that was already there. The smell of burning coal reminded me so much of those cold winter nights in El Sauce with our own *bracero* burning away.

On December 25, 1965, something very special happened. My father, my brother Ulises, and I were baptized at the Intervale Spanish church by Pastor Acosta. My father had started going to church on his own after arriving in New York. He had found the Prospect Spanish church and started attending without ever telling any of us back in Chile. He surprised the whole family when on our first Sabbath in New York City, he took us to church.

We became members of the Washington Spanish church and it became the center of our lives. Church was life for us. It was there that we found friends that embraced, loved, and accepted this South American family. Most of the members were *puertoriqueños* (Puerto Ricans), a most loving, warm, and caring people. There were some days when we did not have much to eat and they would rescue us. On Wednesday nights at prayer meeting, church members would load Mom up with beans, rice, cheese, and other goodies that they preferred not using from their welfare bonuses. Though we were never on welfare, we still benefited from it via our dear friends at the church!

The Washington Spanish church met at a storefront very near to where we lived. We just walked to church. We walked everywhere. The New York City subway and bus system was our means of transportation. We never had a car while I grew up in the Bronx. It was only when my dad found another super's job in Queens that he bought a used car. By then I was away in college. I never had a driver's license till I started working as a pastor in Florida.

The Washington Spanish church gave our family a safe place to grow. It was at that storefront congregation that I found my friends of a lifetime. There I met Lucy Soto, the youth leader. She was a "newyorican" with an attitude. A great attitude! She became my mentor and friend along with her family and brother Angelo, a Vietnam War veteran. He was only a few years older than me and we bonded quite well.

Lucy's father, *el Hermano Soto,* was the patriarch of the church. He provided spiritual leadership for the church and was respected for being *un hombre de Dios* (a man of God). Everyone looked up to him. There were also the Guevaras, Mirta, the choir director, and Pastor Arturo Santos and his family; all of them made a difference in my life. *El Hermano Soto* passed away shortly after we arrived but not before making sure that we found a church building of our own. We bought a Jewish synagogue only a few blocks from the storefront and half a block from the Cross-Bronx Expressway. Then the remodeling of the church started.

Now it was *manos a la obra* (hands to the task)! It was time to get busy and turn the synagogue into a building suitable for our needs. In the evenings and every Sunday, we would gather to remodel. There was no general contractor, no hired hands. It was just us, the members: adults, youth, men and women of all ages and sizes working together to build Jesus a home. During this time, I saw and felt the same energy and passion I had seen back in Chile with my mom and her friends. Now I was experiencing that same spirit as a teenager. It marked me for life. I saw people make sacrifices of time, money, and personal resources. Church was everything! It wasn't just what we "did" together but it was "who" we were. We were a family.

As a family we shared the good, the bad, and the ugly of life. We stuck together through thick and thin. We were there for each other, helping each other, encouraging each other, and meeting each others' needs. It didn't mean that we were *santitos* (holier-than-thou) and had no problems.

We were who we were: needy people. And you know needy people sometimes can be problematic and difficult. Needy people have preferences, things they like and things they don't like. A homeless person is needy, so you bring him a peanut butter and jelly sandwich. Well, he may not like peanut butter and jelly sandwiches, why should we insist on giving him what he doesn't like?

Many of the problems you find in the church are due to people's preferences, not principles. People fight over the color of the carpet, the color of the walls of the sanctuary, music styles, versions of the Bible you read, et cetera. Most of it is just a matter of preference. The apostle Paul describes the church as a body that has members, and these members feel pain and happiness. "Your body has many parts—limbs, organs, cells—but no matter how many parts you can name, you're still one body. ...

"The way God designed our bodies is a model for understanding our lives together as a church: every part dependent on every other part, the parts we mention and the parts we don't, the parts we see and the parts we don't. If one part hurts, every other part is involved in the hurt, and in the healing. If one part flourishes, every other part enters into the exuberance."[1]

The church is a living organism, and as such, it has movement. You can count on it. There's always something happening in the church ... stuff beyond regular church programs. This movement is caused by people. I came to understand this; church and its people were life to me. I saw existence, purpose, family, friends, and

God through the eyes of the church. I wasn't just a member. I was a participant. The kind of life I experienced in church was similar to what Doctor Luke describes in Acts 4:32, 34, "All the believers were one in heart and mind. No one claimed that any of his possessions was his own, but they shared everything they had. … There were no needy persons among them."

What my life in church has taught me is that church is more than a place where you share common doctrinal beliefs with others. It is not about being well-informed. Though beliefs are important and play a significant role in our spiritual formation and growing in the likeness of Christ, they are not everything. I have also learned that church is more than a place where you share a common code of conduct. It is more than just behaving well. It's more than just doing the proper thing and being politically correct. You can be a good person without being a Christian.

I think the church is about belonging. It's about knowing that you have a place there. You may be different in many ways, but you belong there. It's about knowing others deeply and others knowing you deeply. It's about developing long-lasting friendships. The apostle Paul puts it this way, "Now you are the body of Christ, and each one of you is a part of it."[2] This belonging means you play an active role in the life of the church. Church is life for me.

I think God gave us the church so that we would know that we are not alone in our Christian journey. This body that Paul talks about is a group of people coming together, being and working together because they cannot do it alone. The apostle Paul states, "From him the whole body, joined and held together by every supporting ligament, grows and builds itself up in love, as each part does its work."[3]

The church is here so that we will not be alone in our journey. Growing in Christ is not something we do alone, but we grow right along *with* other people. The church is God's way of saying, "I'm with you. I'm with you through your brothers and sisters." These brothers and sisters are here to support and help you as you grow in Christ, and you are here to do the same. They can't do without you, and you can't do without them. We need each other.

Our relationship with God is not just having a *personal* relationship with Him. It is not an *individual* experience. In fact, the Bible doesn't talk about a "personal, individual relationship" with God. The religious experience in the Bible is always lived out in the context of a community of people who share common values and beliefs. It is true that each one of us makes a personal decision to turn our lives over to Christ, but God doesn't leave us there. He brings us to the *ekklesia* so that "we will in all things grow up into him who is the Head, that is, Christ."[4]

The church is a team of people who share a common story: the story of Jesus. They share a common life by becoming Christlike. They share a common mission: telling the story of Jesus to others. Church is a team effort. In soccer, there are eleven players on the field. Though one person scores, there were ten others that contributed to the goal. In basketball, there are six players, and though one person scores, the ball is passed through five other players before it ends up in the hoop of the opposing team.

Not only are there other players but an entire support system of people outside the field or court. There is the coach, medical doctor, assistant coaches, personal trainers, et cetera. Each team is made of people who are there to give all they have for a common cause: WINNING! Even in individual games like tennis, there is a team of people supporting the player. No one plays or competes alone.

Lance Armstrong was asked once what was his secret for winning the three-week Tour de France. His answer: "Never ride alone." You see, Lance is part of the U.S. Postal Team, which is made up of nine riders. The team has one goal in mind: to support the one rider who has the best chance of winning the race. So the team constantly sacrifices itself for the sake of that one rider. They carry food, serve as windbreakers, and ride their bicycles in a way that assures that their leader is never stranded or struggling alone. Whether on a flat road or a fearsome mountain, Lance Armstrong was never alone. He always had team members there to control his pace and keep away those riders who could jeopardize their leader. By keeping close to his team and his team keeping close to him, Lance remained strong throughout the race until he reached the final victory in Paris.

As I think about that walnut tree and the church in the front yard of our house, I cannot help but realize that I was never alone. While growing up I always had people who were there helping me along in my journey in life. In my ministry as a pastor, whether I was cruising in the valley or climbing a steep mountain, I was never alone. You are not alone either. Right where you are, you have your own *ekklesia* to help, encourage, and support you, and *you* are there to help, encourage, and support others. We are all connected. We all belong. You are not alone.

---

1. 1 Corinthians 12:12, 13, 25, 26, *The Message.*
2. 1 Corinthians 12:27.
3. Ephesians 4:16.
4. Verse 15.

The author is an associate director of Youth Ministries for the Florida Conference of Seventh-day Adventists. He writes from Miami.

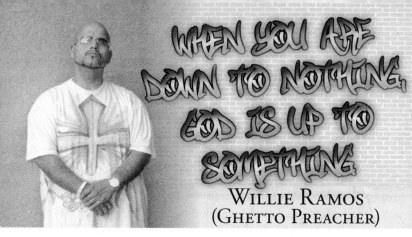

WHEN YOU ARE DOWN TO NOTHING, GOD IS UP TO SOMETHING

WILLIE RAMOS
(GHETTO PREACHER)

That Friday, August 29th, the Holy Spirit was messing with me all day. *"Tomorrow morning, after you preach your sermon,"* He said, *"I want you to make an altar call. But specifically for baptism."*

For baptism? I thought, *No way! You want me to seal the deal? I'm not a closer! Let the pastor do that! Who am I? I'm just a lay preacher.*

You see, that weekend I was the guest speaker at this off-the-chain, big youth event called SDA Rhapsody 003. And as a youth preacher, I have preached dozens of sermons, from L.A. to Canada. I have made plenty of altar calls, but hardly ever for baptisms. So, when God asked me to do it, I got a little bit scared. So, I put it in the back of my head and ignored it.

Sabbath morning, Pastor Manny Cruz, the director of the event and one of my mentors, asked me for a favor. He said, "Yo, Willy. I want you to do something for me. Today, after the sermon, when you do the altar call, can you do it specifically for [Yup. You guessed it!] … baptisms?"

I was like, *Whaaaat?! God, You really want me to do this, huh? OK. I'm going to follow an old Nike slogan and "Just Do It."* Before I tell you the disappointing results, let me tell you a little about myself.

I grew up in a bad neighborhood. It wasn't exactly the PJs (projects), but like Ice Cube said in one of his songs, "I call my neighborhood a ghetto because it houses minorities."

Still, every stereotypical thing that you see in "hood" movies, we had in our block. Drugs, gang bangers, prostitutes, police raids. … And sometimes, on occasions, we would hear the gun blast from some knucklehead's pistol. We also had a rat and roach problem. My brother and I would shoot them with BB guns. Man, if we were smarter, we could've sold those dead rodents to *Fear Factor*! We would've made money!

Anyways, I rolled with a small little crew called TUF (The Ultimate Force). It wasn't hardcore like The Bloods or The Crips, but we were still considered a street gang by the Broward Sheriff's Office.

I became a thief. Sometimes we would jump people for no reason at all. And I became very disrespectful towards my mother. I got kicked out of my crib (house), twice. (I was even homeless for a while!) I got kicked out of school, and I got fired from almost all my jobs for fighting.

Spiritually speaking, I was hellbound. And to top that all off, I was weighing 428 pounds! Now, I weigh 427, I'm losing weight! (*¡No pares, sigue, sigue!*) I was so insecure; I once hit an eight-year-old kid on the head with a baseball bat because he called me fat!

One day, I just felt like ending it all. I felt ugly. (Looking back, I think, *Man, that's a lie straight from the pits of hell, because I'm not ugly!*) I was always the last one to get picked in school to be on any team. If we would play baseball, they would always put me as the catcher … for both teams! That's when you know you're not appreciated! I was short and fat. I looked like the penguin! I was always looking over my shoulder to see if Batman and Robin were going to come tackle me from behind!

But, one day, I just had enough. *I'm going to commit suicide. No one is going to care anyways. I'm useless. I'm a loser.*

That night I went home to grab a gun we had in our house. I started to cry to the God my mama taught me about when I was a young kid. But, it still felt the same. God was ignoring me. It felt as if His answering machine was taking my calls, "I AM not here right now. But, please, leave Me a message."

"GOD!" I cried out, "I need YOU, now! Give me a sign that YOU still love me!"

Still nothing …

Where's God? Where's the Mighty Jehovah?

Have you ever felt that way? Have you ever felt alone? Have you ever heard the silence of Heaven? When you can't hear anything, not even the crickets? Not even the *pollitos* (baby chicks) crying, *"Pío, pío, pío"*?

Nothing.

At least once a week, I check my e-mails, and many times I read from young persons who tell me they feel so alone. They feel that God has abandoned them. They don't feel loved. Some of them have even told me that they cut themselves.

I have felt that way, too. In fact, some of our Bible heroes have felt the same way.

Job (the one who never sinned against God and who "was the greatest man among all the people of the East"[1]) cursed the day he was born.[2]

Elijah begged God to take his life in 1 Kings 19:4. And one of the sons of Korah wrote one of the most depressing songs in the Bible in Psalm 88.

I remember writing a poem just as depressing entitled "Tears of a Clown."

Here it is:

Me … I'm that brother that'll make you laugh
when you feel upset
I walk around like it's all good,
yet I've taken some rough hits.
Man, I'm the life of the party
everybody loves me

people only see my good half,
I see the bad and the ugly.
Still, I'm that brother you can talk to
or that shoulder to cry on.
Hurt me and I'll forgive you
I let bygones be bygones.
I got beef with nobody,
I got a million best friends
if you need me say when
I got your back till the end.
But, at night when I lay down
and there's no one around
I start to cry and only I,
can see the TEARS of a CLOWN.

Have you ever felt this way? Have you ever been overwhelmed by despair like Job and Elijah? If you answered Yes, I have good news …

"I just saved 10 percent on car insurance by switching to Geico!" (Just kidding!) The good news is JESUS CHRIST!

Check out what ended up happening to me that night …

I was so discouraged and tired of crying that instead of killing myself, I fell asleep. Fortunately, the Bible says, "weeping may remain for a night, / but rejoicing comes in the morning."[3]

The next morning, this elderly lady knocked on our door and asked my mother if she had a son. When my mother said Yes, she proceeded to hand her a medallion for me, with a picture of Jesus with His hands opened wide. It seemed He was telling me, "Prodigal son, it's time for you to come back home. I never left you. You left Me." I felt like I was on *Touched by an Angel*! I had never met that lady before in my life! I looked out the window and saw the grey hair on her head. My first reaction was negative, because I always thought my guardian angel looked more like Vin Diesel. Instead, she looked like the old lady from *Titanic*!

But, you know what? Who cares how she looked. God spoke to me that day. The Holy told me, *"No way, José! You are not going to kill yourself on MY watch!"* ' *"For I know the plans I have for you … plans to prosper you and not harm you, plans to give you hope and a future."* ' *'Since you are precious and honored in my sight, / and because I love you.'* "[4]

That is why that morning, I got on my knees and sent God a "knee-mail" entitled "God, I'm sorry! I don't wanna die anymore!" And Jesus quickly replied saying, *"You don't have to die, My main man, for I already died for you."* Amen.

Back to Rhapsody. The stage was set. We had just seen an awesome drama. The praise and worship was great! Two young ladies sang a song that took me straight to the throne of God. All that was needed was for me to do my part. Make a call, "specifically, for baptism." So, I did it.

I must have called out for four or five minutes and nobody was getting up. What had I gotten myself into? I was embarrassed. Then, all of a sudden, two persons got up. Then one more. Then another. A total of seven people got up to get baptized! Praise GOD!

Oh, didn't I say "disappointing results"? Well, I meant for Satan. Jesus Christ was victorious! He is the True Ultimate Force!

So, today I challenge all the youngbloods and anybody else who reads this chapter to trust God. Because, when you are down to nothing, God is up to something! Your comeback is right around the corner. Who knows? Maybe next year I'll be reading your story. I can't wait!

Your TEST can become your TESTimony.
Your MESS can become your MESSage.
And your MISERY can end up as your MINISTRY.
(Author Unknown).

1. Job 1:3.
2. Job 3:1.
3. Psalm 30:5.
4. Jeremiah 29:11; Isaiah 43:4.

The author is a motivational speaker and youth ministry specialist. Learn more about Willie Ramos at: http://www.risingministries.com/ghetto-preacher-willie-ramos.html.

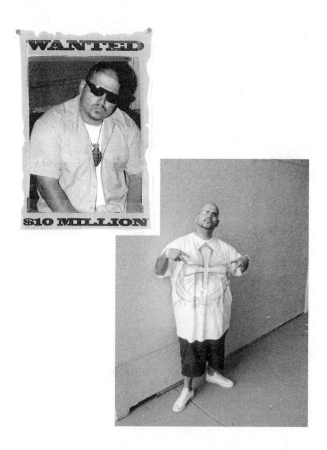

GLOSSARY

(For a complete interactive list, see http://www.urbandictionary.com.)

Barrio: Neigborhood.

Carnal: "Brother" or "sister."

Cholo: A *cholo* usually refers to a Hispanic male that typically dresses in chinos (khaki pants), a sleeveless T-shirt or a flannel shirt with only the top buttoned, a hairnet, or with a bandana around the forehead.

Ese: A fellow Hispanic, a close friend, "homeboy," "dude."

Holmes: What you would call a good friend, a stranger, or can be used in mockery against an adversary.

Homeboy, homie, homegirl: "Friend," member of the same gang.

Jefitos: Means "parents." *Jefita* refers to the mother, and *jefito* to the father.

Mijo: "My son," a contraction of *"mi hijo."*

Paisa: Short term for *paisano,* which translates to "countryman." An inhabitant of a rural or remote area who is usually characterized by an utter lack of sophistication and cultivation.

"Somos pocos pero locos": "We may be few, but we're crazy."

Quinceañera: Celebration of a girl's fifteenth birthday. It is usually a large party, sometimes very ornate and expensive.

Vato: Urban Spanish for "dude" or "man."